MW00977762

The Elected Lady - Finding Victory In The Challenge

*Words of Faith,
Reflections and Inspiration
for Mothers of
Special Needs Children
and Other Moms*

Norma F. Stanley

Outskirts Press, Inc.
Denver, Colorado

The Elected Lady--Finding Victory in the Challenge
Words of Faith, Reflections and Inspiration for Mothers of Special Needs
Children and Other Moms
All Rights Reserved
Copyright © 2007 Norma F. Stanley
V 3.0

Outskirts Press
http://www.outskirtspress.com

ISBN-10: 1-59800-673-8
ISBN-13: 978-1-59800-673-5

Outskirts Press and the "OP" logo are trademarks belonging to
Outskirts Press, Inc.

Printed in the United States of America

WHAT PEOPLE ARE SAYING ABOUT THE ELECTED LADY FINDING VICTORY IN THE CHALLENGE!

"Truly inspirational reading for any mother...a must read!" Twanda Black, radio show host, foster mother of mentally challenged children

"An ingenious way to share God's word with mothers needing healing in their hearts and souls"...Apostle Yolanda Barnett...

"Renews faith in the power of God and a mother's love"....Minister Jackie Moore

"As a youth advocate, I recommend this book as a gift to anyone who cares about the mother of any child, but those with special needs children in particular"...Georgia State Representative, Roger Bruce

TABLE OF CONTENTS

ACKNOWLEDGEMENTS

First of all, I dedicate this book to my Lord and Savior, Jesus Christ, who has brought me a long way from the insecure, shy, easily intimidated, talented, but unproductive people pleaser that I once was. Not only am I no longer any of those things, but my life is becoming above and beyond all that I could ever ask or think.

The Lord took me out of my self bondage and showed me how blessed I truly was and how glorious life could be, if I just believed that it could. He also helped me to begin believing in myself and stir up the gifts that he had given me. So here I am, living, moving and doing for the glory of God and I'm having the time of my life! I thank you God for opening up the windows of heaven and pouring out my blessings. I hope the wisdom in this book and everything you've called me to do and share, will be valuable to others.

I also dedicate this book to women everywhere who in some form or other were chosen to be elected ladies and fight specific challenges, whether they realize it or not. Women like Coretta Scott King and Rosa Parks who have recently transitioned to be with our heavenly father, whose early lives may have begun without fanfare, but whose later life experiences and triumphs have always inspired me and millions of others, to follow in their footsteps. The goal of this being to work at doing all that we could to make necessary changes for others, even as we made changes for ourselves.

I don't exactly know why these two women came to mind when I started to write my dedications, but they did. I do know that when I even thought about writing anything, I was in the sixth grade and the desire to begin writing began right around the time when the Civil Rights Movement was cresting. It was through Ms. Rosa Parks' boldness, courage, obedience and love for God, herself and her culture, that she was able to take the risks that helped change the lives of a multitude of people.

In fact, I was but a child of about nine or ten when I started to hear and learn about the Civil Rights Movement and I had just won an essay competition at our elementary school for the whole sixth grade, about the Movement and Dr. Martin Luther King. I even received a keepsake book as a prize for my achievement sharing information about the Movement, and Dr. King, which I cherished then—and still do. It was just a few weeks later that Dr. King was assassinated.

It was through Mrs. King's struggles with her husband and countless other dedicated warriors involved in the Civil Rights Movement, that I first learned about their determination to obliterate segregation.

Mrs. King and Ms. Parks were two of the many

prominent servants for God who never gave up on their purpose. They dedicated their whole lives to making key changes in the national scene for those of us who were not treated with equal respect and opportunities. They could have, but they didn't let painful and unexpected circumstances keep them from doing what God obviously put them here to do—to initiate and continue the fight for the cause of equal rights for everyone.

I guess in a way, it is for this reason that I wrote this book. Although I can't compare Mrs. King's and Ms. Parks' challenges to the experiences of the women in this book, these women have also been tremendously affected by life and they all share a common reality. They were all especially selected and elected by God to carry out specific assignments that not everyone could complete.

These women are the mothers of mentally and/or physically challenged children, who from the time they learned of their child's disability, have struggled to adjust their lives to see their full development and fulfilling future. They also work to change their communities to ensure their children are provided the respect, acknowledgement and provisions that are afforded to everyone else.

To my young adult daughter, Sierra, a miraculous, wondrous delight, who has made my husband and I the people we have become today. If it weren't for you, I wouldn't have even attempted to write a book and finish it! Even though you were born with your challenges, you teach us every day how awesome our lives really are with your genuinely simple expression of love for everyone, not just your family and friends.

If we could all show more of your qualities and the many children and adults like you with physical and mental challenges—who love simply, live thankfully, explore excitedly, enjoy and revel in the many things so many of us take for granted—what a different place this world would be. Little did I know that bringing you into the world would also give birth to my dreams and change the direction of my life forever—but I thank God that He knew.

To my stepson Steven Jr., who is now a grown man with his own daughter making me a grandma before my time—but that's O.K. by me. Shamaia is a beautiful and smart little girl and you're a great father! I couldn't have asked for a better son, although you gave us you know what growing up—but what teenager doesn't?! I just want you always to remember and relish in the fact that for those who believe, life gets better and better as we all get older and wiser.

To my husband Steven, who has been the love of my life since I was 14. Yes, we are totally different in personality as day is from night, and despite all our tussles, we have had a wonderful marriage that's happily lasted over 20 years. Thank you for being there and supporting me in all of my various ventures as I searched for my identity…I'm sure you thought I was nuts, but you let me explore and hung in there with me anyway and it's paying off in ways we could have only imagined. Now, you're what I call a chosen man!

To both my moms--my birth mother Evelyn Osborne, and my mother-in-law, Mary Stanley, who both taught me how to use my innate strength and resolve to make the best life that I could for my children. With me having no clue, you taught me what needed to be done in terms of raising children and having a family and how and to do it, just by observing you both.

I want to also say thank you to my true friends, sisters and brothers (biologically and in Christ) who supported my dreams and prayed with me—even when you didn't understand those dreams. To Janet, Laurette, Zelma, Marilyn, Dwayne---thanks for being there for my family when we needed you.

And to Bonita, my long time hang-out buddy. We've known each other since before Sierra was born and as we move onto new seasons of our lives, I'm sure we'll have much to celebrate in the areas about which we've always dreamed and to which we were pre-destined.

To Yolanda, thanks for praying for me, encouraging me and spiritually guiding me all these years. I learned a lot from you. I'm glad to see you've met your Boaz and that what you've believed about all of our futures is coming to pass.

Aside from my husband, I would like to thank one of my best friends, Helga Moore, who is also a part of this book. The mother of a special needs child like I am, Helga and I have only known each other just a few short years, yet we have developed a familial bond and kinship like sisters.

Just like with my real sisters, we look out for each other.

Helga, we've had a successful and productive four years knowing that the key to our future rests in God, knowing that all children *are* special, that we are elected ladies finding victory in the challenge, and that our "Jobetta," days are not only behind us but before us, making us Stronger!

And of course, I absolutely must thank all the other elected ladies, who participated in and who inspired this book. The majority of these women are mothers of special needs children and one special elected lady who was once a special needs child.

A special thanks to Bishop Eddie L. Long, senior pastor of New Birth Missionary Baptist Church. You inspired me to become a "dream girl" and go after my hopes, my dreams and pursue my destiny. You also helped me realize that we don't choose destiny, but that destiny chooses us. Thank God, I'm moving in my destiny.

Thank you all for your time, your honesty, your prayers and your faith. God loves you all and so do I.

FOREWORD

You are about to read a unique book by a special woman--a woman, who has experienced the love and has insight into the workings of our Lord. "The Elected Lady-Finding Victory in the Challenge," is a book which clearly shows how we all, but a special group of women in particular, are sometimes elected by God to face challenges and take on responsibilities that we would, most likely, have never chosen for ourselves.

In accepting the responsibility and rising to the occasion, these women have come to understand and appreciate that the challenge was really a portal of personal growth. And, in taking on these challenges, they have not only undergone remarkable changes in themselves, but have equally changed the lives of those who have come into their presence or the multitudes who have been exposed to their stories.

This is not only a story of challenge and sacrifice, but a story of love--a mother's love. Not only her love for her family, but the greatest of familial love, the love for her child. That the children, themselves are mentally or physically challenged is all the more poignant. For we justly come to learn in this book, that often God's challenges in life are truly blessings in disguise.

Sit back and prepare to be moved, as Norma Stanley author of "The Elected Lady-Finding Victory in the Challenge," passionately shares the strength of these mothers, their strong beliefs and faith in God, the pain they've experienced, the obstacles facing their children and then the joy of overcoming self doubt and finding peace. Come join in the revelation of what life and love are truly about. I know you will love the outcomes, as have I.

Captain William "T" Thompson, Esq.
January, 2007

INTRODUCTION

This book is especially written for women and mothers of children born with physical and mental disabilities, although the messages within, I believe, will appeal to all women. However, the purpose of this book is to shed light on many of the women with disabled children, who in our society are taken for granted, overlooked, and underestimated...just as their children are.

Amazing women are found everywhere, but the mothers of special needs children are unsung heroines who are overshadowed, and I'd like to bring focus to some of their struggles and how they are coping with their challenges.

"The Elected Lady—Finding Victory in the Challenge—Words of Faith, Reflections and Inspiration for Mothers of Special Needs Children and Other Moms," is a primarily autobiographical book, especially designed to help women facing the challenge of raising and caring for a special needs child, to discover their vast potential. It also offers positive life lessons shared through a few women who are surmounting this daunting task.

It was written to help mothers like these, discover the strong, powerful, loving, determined and significant person within, learning how and when to use and display these "super" powers God placed in them from the beginning of time. In addition, the purpose of this book is to ensure women with special needs children are choosing to successfully reflect, regroup, rebound and even rejoice about the sometimes uncertain path their life has taken.

I am praying that this book will touch the many elected ladies out there, who are struggling to understand, tackle and overcome their individual challenges. And to realize that no matter what, they need to continue to seek and hear God whisper words of love in their ears so they can do the same for their children.

Please note, that except for Helga, Kate and myself, the names of the other women described within, were changed to protect their privacy. However, the book allows readers to identify closely with one or more of them.

"To the elect lady and her children, whom I love in truth, and not only I, but also all those who have known the truth."

2 John1:1

CHOSEN WOMEN

We reflect on our past, envision our future
Encumbered by pain, at times cushioned by
pleasure
Hearts enraptured in our children's eyes
Always loving them beyond measure
Yet we know not too many could live our lives,
Walk our walk or run our race
Not wanting to think much about the days and
nights we face
Yet determined to do more than necessary to reach
beyond the place
Where only our Lord Jesus and Father God can
hear
Where our angels bathed in white light, stay near
Believing what God designed is so much more than
we can see
Where strength, hope, faith and love reflect all
we're meant to be
Yes, weeping may endure for a night, but joy does
come in the morning
Until then, we pray the poison and pain are
extracted from the sting
For another day to live, laugh, dance and sing
We were chosen for battles and victories we can not
yet see
But we're not afraid, because we will reach our
destiny!

Chapter One
Chosen Women

"But you are a chosen generation, a royal priesthood, a holy nation, His own special people, that you may proclaim the praises of Him who called you out of darkness into His marvelous light...1 Peter 2:9

There are many chosen and elected women in the bible selected to do some awesome things, but Esther is one of my favorites. Her life was filled with faith and bravery, as well as the willingness to take life-endangering risks for others, risks not many would have taken. Her love and compassion for her people, faithfulness to God and her courage to endure whatever she had to, truly inspired me and should be an inspiration to all of us. I tend to read that chapter more often than many of the others, because in the end, Esther became a renowned chosen woman throughout the centuries.

I read the book of Esther most often because I admire the way she handled her frightening situation. She didn't know what her future held, but she was willing to put herself on the line, and possibly sacrifice her life for others. Esther was courageous, caring, concerned and committed to change. Her goal was to protect the lives of her people and she used her influence and intelligence to help those who couldn't help themselves. In a way, that is what this book is all about.

One of my most motivating and cherished verses among many in the book of Esther is, "Yet who knows whether you have come to the Kingdom, for such a time as this?" (Esther 4:14).

Although we may not have come across the dangerous challenges Esther faced in saving her whole nation from destruction, I do believe it is our roles as mothers of special needs children, to take on the responsibility of fighting negative perspectives and treatment of our children.

I also believe that as mothers of these children, we were especially selected by God in this life and this purpose "for such a time as this."

As much as we would like to think so, we were not chosen for our lot in life by chance or by mistake, because I believe God doesn't make mistakes. It wasn't just rotten luck or happenstance. The challenges we encounter, assignments we've undertaken, misfortunes we've suffered through, as well as the achievements we've made, were all part of God's predetermined plan for our lives.

Sometimes, part of His plan is very painful and I'm sure I can speak for many—both women and men--when I say that at the time of these individual experiences, we very much wanted to bury our heads (and sometimes our bodies) in the sand and never come out again.

Unfortunately, many parents of special needs children take drastic measures to deal with the pain, sometimes abusing themselves and others, including their children, because they didn't have enough faith in themselves or in God, His love and covering, or the unique task with which He had entrusted them.

And believe me, there are many very painful moments, like having a young adult daughter on her menstrual cycle without the capacity to care for herself. I thank God for prescribed injections for that! I'm strong, but I know I'm not that strong! Another example of the challenges many of us face, is cleaning them if they can't use the bathroom on their own. Most parents like my husband and I get used to it and after a while it doesn't even phase us anymore. But there are others who never get used to the not too pleasant experience.

But there are some very joyful, happy times also for those who don't give up right a way. For those who do, they never get the chance to experience the many opportunities to jump and shout with incredible joy, for the small yet consistent steps their children were making--even if those moments came intermittently or later than normal in most children's lives.

Things like seeing their children start to talk at 10 years-old or older—or walk even if it's with a walker. How about experiencing their getting out of diapers at 12 (or older), something with which my husband and I are still challenged. Then there's teaching them (with the help of their occupational therapy sessions), to feed themselves by learning how to use their hands, fingers and utensils properly.

Although Sierra, now a young adult, has wonderful comprehension and follows instructions in many areas, she still doesn't talk in full sentences, but learns new words daily. She can't say certain letters too well beginning with "m"—except for "Mommy", "Ma", and "Mom," and she also has trouble with words that begin with "s", so she pronounces her name "ierra," instead of Sierra.

Of course, she can say "Daddy," but the words she says the most are "work", "bus" and "usic," which we know means music, as well as "eat", her favorite word of all! Others may not understand the special language she speaks, but we do. She loves to sing nursery rhymes and Happy Birthday, by humming the tunes, which she does very well. In addition, she loves contemporary gospel music and tries to sing along with her favorite singers like CeCe Winans, Kirk Franklin, Jay Moss, and me, her mom!

We're also very blessed and excited to see that she is starting to take a few steps without us holding her hand or using her walker, and we're extremely happy about that! We practice walking and taking steps with her daily for about five minutes a day, and afterward, she's huffing and puffing as if she's run a marathon, but she likes to do it over and over again.

It seems she is determined to walk and even tries to walk up the stairs holding on to the banister with just one hand. Although I'm right behind her, I really don't encourage it because I'm afraid she'll try it when I'm not around and hurt herself—but inside I'm jumping for joy!

These are things parents like us get excited about and are just a few of the many milestones etched in the minds and hearts of mothers (and fathers) with these special children. However brief or long lasting these moments and memories are, mothers of physically and mentally challenged children want to share their happiness (sometimes tearfully) with the world.

Life can throw us so many twists, turns and unexpected curves and it takes very special, unique, feisty and determined women, to stand and withstand what is thrown at us. Yet, because God created us and guides our steps along the way, He knew that we could handle it, even though at times, we didn't think we could. Once we do realize it however, it is incredible to see how much God thought of us to choose us specifically for this unique, difficult task and this seemingly never ending journey.

No matter where you may find yourself in this journey, you must understand that just as with other parents, we've all been through the ringer and many phases of parenting. But parenting a special needs child is different, and in a majority of cases, instead of pining, whining and wallowing in depressions, for the most part, we tend to handle it all patiently and courageously. As a result, we are more confident, stronger and more determined women than we were when we came into this role.

For any woman, it is not easy to wake up one day and find yourself living a life and walking a path that you would never have chosen for yourself, yet, so many of us do. Women in general eventually have no choice but to finally wake up from their little girl fantasies of their knights in shining armor—or Kens to their Barbie's, coming to their rescue and taking them off to live in mansions, happily ever after.

When we do wake up, most of us are not prepared for the rough hand life has dealt us. Some of us move through these stages of life rebelliously-- kicking and screaming, full of anger and resentment, causing additional trauma for ourselves, and still others move through life in zombie-like states not allowing themselves to feel either joy or pain.

However, as much as we'd like to, we can't escape it. We were chosen to carry out our assignments as it relates to the disability community and our communities' acceptance of them as valuable contributors to our society--beginning with our own children.

Over the years, the many battles we've fought

and victories we've won were by no means allowed for us to experience without reason. They were to teach us about ourselves, who we truly were inside. These lessons were carefully orchestrated, strategically planned and skillfully designed for our good and for God's glory. Today I can truly thank God for my lessons, no matter how painful some of them may have been.

The prophet Jeremiah said, in Jeremiah 29:11-14 "For I know the thoughts that I think toward you, says the Lord, thoughts of peace and not of evil to give you a future and a hope. Then you will call upon Me and go and pray to Me and I will listen to you. And you will seek Me and find Me, when you search for Me with all our heart. I will be found by you, says the Lord, and I will bring you back from your captivity."

This is so true because for too many of us, we don't think to seek out God *until* we find ourselves in trouble, facing some crisis or are on the brink of some disaster. I know that was particularly true in my case. Although I've always been a Believer, I didn't really get to know who God or Jesus was until I faced my own real crisis—the birth of our beautiful daughter, Sierra, who was born with cerebral palsy.

Assignments By God Are Sometimes Unexpected

It wasn't until I was married about five years, that we found out we were going to have a baby. Always an avid reader, it seemed I read almost every book there was about preparing to parent a child and thought I'd done everything right and had everything under control. That was until I gave birth to my baby daughter Sierra, at which time both my husband and I were about 30-years-old.

It wasn't until nine months later that I was told she was developmentally delayed—although I had suspected months ago that something was a little off, because she wasn't developing according to what the books said. But our pediatrician didn't seem concerned, saying that all babies grow at their own pace, so we didn't worry and went about our daily lives.

About the time Sierra was a year old, her developmentally delayed status was changed to cerebral palsy, a condition we learned more about after this diagnosis.

At first I cried until I couldn't cry anymore. I kept asking myself "What happened? How could this be?" As far as I knew, I'd done all the right things. I had never taken any drugs and took all the right vitamins and other pre-natal pills prescribed. I was always on time for my monthly check-ups and did exactly what the doctor said.

In fact, I only gained 17 pounds and that should

have been a clue that something was wrong, because most pregnant women I knew had gained at least 25 pounds, however, at the time our doctor said there was nothing to worry about.

My delivery was more than a bit terrifying, but not as painful as I had imagined. After seeing that film in sex education class in high school, I was absolutely terrified at the prospect of giving birth. Never the less, I delivered a beautiful baby girl seven hours after arriving at the hospital. At first, Sierra seemed perfectly fine.

Yet, here we were with a year-old baby girl who the doctors said would now be limited in her physical and mental development. I refused to accept that diagnosis although it hurt quite a bit at first—actually it took me a few months to recover from the shock, but no matter how many doctors supposedly verified what her pediatrician and neurologist had said, I chose to believe God.

So while I continued to work in my corporate executive job during the day, taking time off a few times a week to take Sierra to various therapists, I soon realized this wasn't going to work.

I was a public relations professional and had over 15 years of working at wonderful companies and agencies. For example, I was a director of corporate communications for several years in the headquarters of a major fast food restaurant. This was a job I loved. It was, in fact, when I was working there that I gave birth to Sierra. However, when it moved its corporate headquarters to Florida,

I chose not to go with them and began doing some freelancing.

These contract PR consulting positions turned into executive positions in a few nationally renowned marketing and public relations firms and I enjoyed them all, as I worked around Sierra's therapies.

However, I soon realized that I either had to choose between my fast-paced career (which at the time I loved), or the well-being of my daughter, so you know which one I chose. I left corporate America and never looked back, (at least, not too often).

This was more than 15 years ago and it was where tremendous faith stepped in, which to tell you truthfully, took more than a while to develop. I didn't know it then, but I was one of God's "chosen" women.

Chosen not only to make an impact on my immediate and extended family in evangelizing to them, but also to everyone I had or had not yet met, who needed the benefit of what my life testimonies could offer. It was then that I realized that the experiences, gifts and talents God gave me were for a specific purpose, although at the time, I had no idea what that purpose was.

I found out more than 10 years later, that my assignment was to change the perception and care of physically and mentally challenged people, through other children and their parents. These were people who had not personally experienced this situation and didn't know how to handle being around the mentally and physically challenged. While most are sympathetic, they didn't begin to understand how or why people were disabled or understood how they could relate positively to this community.

I have to admit there was a time when I was a child, I was the same. I was a little unsure of interacting with people with physical and mental disabilities, those who others would call "retarded." That, however, never stopped me from trying to keep the bullies away from a mentally disabled boy I grew up with in East Harlem, New York.

Junior was his nickname and it was my first experience with interacting with the mentally challenged. At first I was extremely uncomfortable around him—I was around 11 at the time, but shortly realized that he was just a kid (although a big strapping kid), who wanted to play, just like all the other kids did, so I played with him.

Then there was Lamar who wore metal leg braces, and who was a comedian who played basketball with my husband Steven and all the guys when they were all young teens, and he thought of himself as a player with the girls. I got to know Lamar when Steven and I began courting, as they called it back then, and found him to be a lot of fun. I noticed he kind of hopped when he walked, but it didn't bother me at all and I never paid it much attention. I guess I was growing more mature.

I also remember two single mothers who were

Hispanic with mentally challenged children—a boy and girl respectively. I remember watching these mothers take care of their children, putting them on the special school bus, taking them grocery shopping and I remember I hardly ever saw these women smile. They always seemed tired and sad and my heart went out to them.

I didn't know it then, but perhaps God was preparing me for what I would face with my own daughter and my own future.

Preparation and experience are keys to success of any major undertaking, and just as my keys of preparation unlocked certain doors in my life, such were the keys that unlocked the doors for Helga, Debbie, Kate, Elizabeth and Jennifer. We all handled our challenges of parenting our special needs child in different ways, or in Kate's case growing up and becoming an adult with physical challenges of her own. But we all faced our futures individually and head on.

As chosen women of God assigned to our own special situations, I'd like to share some perspectives of women including myself, who realized that no matter how prepared we all thought we were for life, we were in no way prepared for this particular challenge, but we managed to handle it because love overcame our fear.

Helga, for example, is a fighter and a chosen woman if there ever was one. When it comes to her children—particularly her son—she takes no prisoners. A dear friend, minister and former housewife, Helga is the mother of two beautiful, strong, determined and talented daughters who are on their way to securing their own individual success. However, Moses, her strapping young adult mentally challenged son, was born with Agenesis of the Corpus Colosum, meaning a piece of his brain is missing, but he and her daughters, are the essence of her life.

Whether she realized it or not, it was evident to all who've been in her presence, either in the past or presently, that despite the various circumstances she faced, ones which would have made most women (and many men) run for the hills, Helga took life's lumps with stride.

Despite her many adversities, Helga was determined to stay faithful to God and drew on this strength. She held on to His spirit and His peace to do what she had to do. Inwardly, she knew she had been called to raise her son Moses and care for other special needs children, through her at-home care service for parents of special needs children. Through this home care service, Helga provided respite services for parents who needed a break and she developed unique ways of working with the children, helping other mothers like herself, but she knew there was more to do.

In order to fully execute her purpose and calling, Helga had to give up her own comfort and stability to strike out into new territory. Although she knew it would be difficult, she was determined to work towards developing her vision to create programs and services. Services that would change the mostly inadequate systems in place for working mothers with special needs children. Not only would these services help the children of these other mothers, but she and her son Moses, as well.

Helga (and many other elected ladies) is not unlike those found in the bible who endured and overcame adversity, sacrificed much and went to any length for the sake of their children. Let's take Jochebed for instance, Miriam and Moses' mother who sent Moses away on the River Nile to keep him from being killed, only to have him be raised by another woman.

Maybe it's no coincidence that Helga's son is also named Moses, because in order to accomplish what she had to do to make life better for herself, for him and other children like him, she let him live with another family. Even for a while, this was a major sacrifice and an excruciatingly, painful thing for her to do.

"I had to put my pain aside and let another family help me with Moses when he became an adult, so I could embark on a path of which I was more than a little uncertain. As painful and scary as that was, I knew I had to do it not only for the well-being of my son, but the well being of other mothers with children like mine. I was uncertain of my future, but the only thing I did know was that I was being led in another direction by a powerful spirit within me and I couldn't ignore it.

I was terrified striking out on my own, without the support of the family and friends I was used to, but I knew there were some things I had to leave behind, and others that I had to reach for, or I wouldn't be able to achieve what I believed deep inside I could. So, I set out on what I knew was unchartered territory...at least for me.

I didn't know what I was getting into when I founded All Children Are Special, a non-profit organization created to develop an all-encompassing facility providing working parents of special needs children a host of necessary services including childcare, that doesn't exist in the disability communities across the nation. We still have a long way to go, but I'm very thankful that we're moving closer to what I envisioned and what God was leading me to every day.

Still in the early development stages, with the help of a few influential community leaders, the development of our Center is moving forward and we're extremely excited about its future possibilities. There is so much to this vision, and it's a daunting task, but somebody's got to do it and it seems as if God had chosen me for that assignment.

I guess my background and experience as a child in some way prepared me for the reality of mothering and providing care for special needs children. One day, God brought back to mind a little boy I had befriended, who I used to take care of and who was also mentally challenged. I've always loved taking care of babies and because he

15

lived with us for a while, I took care of him.

I don't know why I took to him the way I did, but I loved him and actually loved taking care of Bobby, until he was sent to live with another family. But I always remembered that he needed and responded to a lot of love and attention, and not too many people knew how or even wanted to share those things with him. Perhaps that was God's way of getting me ready for my life today, but the journey most certainly has not been easy.

Because it seems that God is the ultimate multi-tasker, I've learned that He sometimes gives us more than one thing to do at the same time, helping to show us what we can and can not do—all the while guiding us through the whole process. That was definitely the case with me.

Although my childhood and early adult life was full of mishaps, hardships, disappointments and even abuse those experiences turned into intense training for the woman I am today and are leading me to where I'm going tomorrow.

I do believe part of God's purpose for me is to minister to women who've been through some of what I've been through. These experiences ran the gamut for me, including becoming a mother to, and raising a son with disabilities, all while fighting for my self worth and my own dreams.

Prayerfully, sharing all this will help women like me find there's some hope in their lives, some dignity and a reason to respect and love themselves and their special needs children—because we all deserve love and respect, and I know God wants us all to have it."

Kate is another chosen woman, who I find incredibly inspiring and for whom I have enormous admiration and respect. She was born with cerebral palsy and outpaces anyone who tries to keep up with her. She lives a full and adventurous life, enlightening and amazing those in her midst with her boldness and her many accomplishments. A local and national disability community advocate and consultant, Kate has never let challenges of growing up with cerebral palsy deter her from anything, including her life's mission.

"I am used to life's challenges and overcoming them, because I won't let anything or anyone stop me from going after my goals. I also won't allow others with similar challenges keep themselves from living full lives, if there is any way I can. I've had a full and blessed life because I was determined to do so. Not only have I been married twice, but I am the mother to a son born with no physical or mental challenges; and I have been blessed to experience what many without disabilities have yet to enjoy.

One of the areas of which I am most proud, is that I have been able to use my life experiences to work with organizations all around the world, with the goal of improving the conditions for and increasing the resources available to the disability community.

I believe my assignment in life is to serve as an

17

example of what people can accomplish with physical limitations, in spite of what others think. I was born with a triple whammy...being female, African American and with physical challenges. However, I've learned that the struggles we face in life have a specific purpose. As far as my disability goes, that turned out to be a two-edged sword.

Sometimes it works in my favor and sometimes it doesn't. For instance, in many cases people sometimes have lower expectations of me because of my physical challenges of not being able to walk, but at the same time, they are also surprised at my achievements. Even though it wasn't exactly what I had planned, I do believe that I'm one of the women God chose to serve as an example of why others shouldn't put limitations on people with disabilities;, because just like anyone else, with a little faith, hard work and support, we have the potential to do more than even we think.

Debbie, the mother of two young adult sons doesn't know if one of her sons, Terrance, being born with cerebral palsy, was an assignment from God or not, but she has accepted it and persevered.

"I think God expects us to take whatever we've been given and do the best we can with it. Now, do I think He actually chose me for this assignment, I don't know, but I do know that not everyone can handle tough situations like this and rise to the occasion.

I am proud to say that not only did I rise to the

occasion, but I believe that I have done an excellent job of raising my son to be an independent and positive young man. So maybe, in a way, I was chosen by God to do this."

"When God selects you for His blessing and favor, although your circumstance may require some long suffering, know your position is powerful, your loving is lasting, and heaven bound is your spirit."

THE BATTLE ISN'T OURS

Dismayed and disappointed when reality hits
We're ready to fight with our hearts, with our fists
No one can feel our hurt and our pain
We look out the window and all we see is rain
We used to laugh with joy at even the little things
But instead of laughter, tears fall when hearing
*   birds sing*
Our swords are sharpened with our tongue
Unwittingly defensive around anyone and everyone
Lashing out at our fortune in life,
Not believing that this too shall pass
We suffer in silence wondering just how long this
*   will last*
Then one day from our hearts we hear a still voice
*   say*
That we're safe in His arms, not to worry,
Because the battle isn't ours—it's the Lord's.
So ignore what those who don't understand say,
Drop your sword, dry your tears and continue to
*   pray*

Chapter Two
The Battle Isn't Ours

"Thus says the Lord to you: Do not be afraid or dismayed of this great multitude, for the battle is not yours, but God's." 2 Chronicles 20:21

Staying faithful and positive through adversity is not the easiest thing in the world to do. One minute life is going well, or at least we're able to handle the occasional mishaps, and the next, Wham! We're blindsided, hit with a knock down drag out punch we didn't see coming.

As I shared earlier, I was one of the thousands of women, who didn't see giving birth to a special needs child on the horizon. As a means of trying to comfort myself, I began looking for others and to others, who may have also been left almost immobile by this devastating news, so I wouldn't feel so alone. Again, I went to the bible for reference, because at the time, I didn't feel I could turn to anything or anyone else. I felt I was at the edge and didn't know what to do. In the bible I found stories of two women whose life challenges kind of stayed with me, because of their sudden devastation. These were two examples, however there, yet there are many, many more.

Naomi was one, who despite having her husband and sons killed in battle, lost everything, her wealth and her home, but never gave up on her faith, although her sadness sometimes overwhelmed her. In fact, despite her own worries, through her love for others and wisdom, she even helped one of her daughters-in-law, the ever-loyal Ruth, to pick up the pieces from her own tragic circumstances and after a while of even more struggle, move on to lead a loving, prosperous and blessed life.

Then there was Susanna, a married woman of wealth, who was faithful to her husband and in her belief in God. Then her life changed. She was suddenly faced with being stoned to death because of two old men who saw her bathing tried to bribe into having sex with them, or they would accuse her of adultery (yes, they even did things like that back in bible days)! The penalty for actions like that back then, was death. Although it could have cost her life, she chose to scream for help instead of giving in and prayed until God delivered her through the help of a young man named Daniel.

Those two women stayed with me because it proved to me that God does fight your battles for you and is always with you, even if sometimes you can't tell that He is. After a while, you come to expect the unexpected, and realize that no matter how well you plan for things, and no matter how well your life is seemingly going—there will be obstacles to climb and fights to fight. This is all a part of life; but it's good to know that God has got your back and gives you strength, when you can no longer fight.

Although every case is unique, having a child born with a disability is most certainly an adversity and a battle most women like me would have preferred not to fight.

However, once that challenge appeared, we had no choice but to take it (with God's help) through to the finish, and some of us are yet still in the battle.

Finding out about our children's disabilities may have been extremely painful at first, but eventually it helped us all to find out what kind of people we really were. Were we cowards or were we fighters? Were we quitters or were we winners? In reality, we really couldn't tell or didn't know for sure, until our backs were against the wall and we found we had little choice but to wind our way through the maze. And we continue to do so, every day, little by little, one fight at a time.

As for me, whatever ignorance and insensitivity I may have had in the matter, disappeared quickly after Sierra was born. It brought back to my remembrance the women with their own disabled children. God showed me how difficult a time those women must have had, and how they just kept on going, no matter how challenging their circumstances may have been. As a result, I knew I had no excuse but to do the same.

God also showed me that this was my chance to be of service, to make a difference in situations like mine. I realized that by putting my compassion, background, abilities and tenacity to work, I could try to change things by caring enough—not just for my child, but for other children and parents in the same situation.

As it turned out, the most difficult battle I had ahead of me was finding who I really was, which to tell the truth, I wasn't sure I wanted to know. One thing I did know was that from early adolescence, I tried to make positive, solid decisions through adulthood, which kept me out of trouble. So I was very confused about the outcome.

I earned good grades and graduated with honors from college. I even avoided sexual temptations (even though there were some awfully cute guys in college)!

I got a good entry level job at a major advertising firm and continued to be promoted up the professional and financial ladder. I even married my husband Steven (my high school sweetheart), in my mid-twenties.

So you can imagine how very angry I was that things turned out not to be not as perfect as I had hoped and planned. I was now the mother of a special needs child…and wondered how could this be?—it just wasn't fair! Well, I learned very quickly that life wasn't fair, so I had to get over my self pity party and move on.

I had never been a quitter and I wasn't about to

become one now. I cried for awhile, then regrouped and came out ready to take on whatever and whomever I had to, to do what I had to do for my daughter's future.

Although at first, I felt that my husband and I were all alone in this crisis, it wasn't long before I found out there were many other families in the same predicament. We all wanted to do whatever we could to maximize the opportunities for our children, but didn't know to whom to turn or where to go. There were peer groups, where families got together and discussed their challenging experiences.

Those groups helped many couples, but for us, those just weren't working. So after a few sessions we stopped attending them.

I remained a bit angry for a while and found myself becoming cryptic, sarcastic and not someone others wanted to be around—not even my husband. Again, I just turned the whole situation over to God. Not by nature a confrontational, aggressive person, I was surprised that I seemed ready to always question things and was not as trusting in accepting what "experts" had to say.

A new side of me began to emerge, which I know only God could bring out. This was a side of me ready and positioned to stand. I was ready and willing to take on the bureaucracy handling our family crisis, and others in our predicament. As a parent of a special needs child and as a reporter, I started to investigate why things were the way they were and how I could fix them. All I had to do was hear that inner voice telling me what to do and when to do it.

I must admit though, I had to listen for His direction closely, because it seemed many a time, He took too long to respond to my questions and to my prayers. He took way too long to respond to my questions and to my prayers. I wanted to take care of things myself, which in most cases wouldn't have been wise. Situations like seriously considering knocking out a para-professional in the schools' disability education, who wasn't paying attention and my pretty daughter fell while running with her walker on cement, putting two gashes in her chin, needing stitches. This happened on her second day of summer school and as you can imagine, Sierra's dad and I weren't too happy with this so-called "professional."

I'm certainly glad I listened that time, and calmed myself down (at least for the most part), because jumping the gun (or even thinking of using one), would have caused me much more harm than good. But it's the way mothers like me feel much of the time. Not just in that case, but in many others, I learned to squash feelings like that, because for the sake of my daughter, I didn't need to shut any doors God was trying to open.

So I learned to wait as patiently as possible for that voice. I turned my attention to raising Sierra. My husband and I saw to it that she had a loving, happy, normal, fun and safe environment in which to grow. One of the battles Steven and I kept running into, however, was finding trustworthy, dependable care for her for after school when we had engagements to attend, had to work late or just wanted to get away for a date every now and then.

Unfortunately, it wasn't until she was about 14-years-old that we found out there was something called respite services. This is where individuals were trained to take care of children like Sierra to give parents a break—and I found this out through word of mouth, not through the programs or professionals who were supposed to share this information, which could have really taken some of the pressure off of us occasionally. I actually learned about it from my friend, Helga.

Of course, until I myself needed them, I didn't take much notice to the large number of needed services for families with children like mine. Although they do care and want to help, I've discovered that many of the representatives of these organizations have never personally experienced situations like ours, as parents, so they really didn't understand our dilemmas. As a result, in many cases, they made wrong decisions, making things worse.

Among the challenges mothers with special needs children face are not necessarily where we are fighting the system, but fighting our emotions. Our inability to at times, overcome depression about things other parents take for granted. This is a major obstacle for some of us to get through and get past.

For me, it was something as simple as knowing your child has no cognizance of the Christmas holidays, which brought on feelings of despair. In my opinion, one of the more trying times of being a parent of a mentally challenged child is watching your child during the Christmas holidays and knowing they have no idea of what it means.

Sierra didn't really begin appreciating Christmas until a few years ago when she was about 14. She now gets up early (which she does all the time anyway), and goes to look at the lights on the tree and starts tearing open gifts. But there was a time, from four years old and older, that she barely noticed the tree. It was a very painful for me to wake her up way past the break of dawn when other children were rushing to see what they got for Christmas, realizing that she didn't understand it all.

That was an extremely hard time for me.

Then there are times when just having children ask your child to play with them, becomes so important to you. I've experienced this many times in the park or at the home of friends or associates. Because the children are not encouraged by their parents to do so, children without any disabilities seem to never even consider inviting our children to play with them. Seeing what may seem like something so small to other parents, instills a tremendous amount of joy for parents with special needs children. Unfortunately though, this happens too few and far between.

This probably comes from the discomfort many

people feel when around physically and mentally challenged people—no matter if they're children or adults. I remember what that felt like, because I was there once, but I would think compassion would overrule discomfort, but found that's not necessarily the case.

I remember keenly, one afternoon when we were at a barbecue and the kids were running back and forth on the lush green yard in back and none of the children thought to ask her to play—they didn't even look her way. Sierra sat on the ground of the cement patio and just watched them running back and forth, because she couldn't walk; but I could see the desire to play and sad look in her eyes. Maybe that was just me wishing she could be part of it, but it was another of the many painful experiences I had as her mother.

She didn't have any young cousins around to play with her—they all lived in other states, so her father and I did what we could to make up for it all by playing with her for long periods of time at home or taking her to the park to get on the swings and the other playground equipment on which she could play.

Sierra loved the swing. The one with the little enclosed seat for small children; we would swing her back and forth time after time after time—after time, until she grew too big for it. She also loved sandboxes—we'd get in quite a mess playing with her in those sand boxes, and got some strange looks from parents seeing grown people in the children sandboxes, but she loved it, so we loved it too.

Putting her on the slide was kind of fun and funny for all of us.

Steven and I would take turns-- one would climb up the steps with her and the other would catch her as she slid to the bottom. Taking turns climbing and catching Sierra took many hours at the park, because Sierra wanted to do it all day long and we tried to keep going for as long as we could, but we were pooped out after about 20 or 30 rounds. She had lots of fun with that, until she outgrew getting on the slide because her legs (and body) had gotten too long.

In a way, it was a blessing that Sierra, an ever-happy child, didn't dwell on negative experiences, even if she noticed them at all, which we don't think she did. But seeing her joy in those small things, and her expression of love for us, quickly helped us to get past what could have also been a sad time.

In fact, Sierra is a very fortunate child, because we were able to take her places and do things with her that her other younger cousins have yet to see and experience. She was able to go to places like Disney World, plays, museums and she seemed to enjoy herself. However, there's nothing that can take the place of just playing and being around other kids. All children need to feel as if they are part of the bunch—not necessarily just special needs kids. However, you can't really blame the children who don't really know any better and invite our children to play.

Much of this behavior comes from the lack of education and in some cases, the lack of compassion they see in their parents. The fact of the matter is that children only mirror what they see and learn from their parents and home environments, which is a shame. It's one of the things I'm hoping to help change.

Fighting While Wounded

I may have thought I had it rough as Sierra was growing up, but truthfully, my experiences were nothing in comparison to what my friends were facing.

Women like Elizabeth, Jennifer, Helga and Debbie had faced situations, truths, trials and tribulations as mothers of special needs children, young adults or even children with no indication of any disability, that were enough to make most people put down their weapons and surrender to the enemy—but they didn't.

For example, Elizabeth was a mother of three wonderful children, one of whom was a perfectly fine, popular high school honor student about to graduate. Then the inexplicable and unimaginable happened. There was no sign that there was anything wrong, when her oldest daughter was diagnosed with a brain tumor, after passing out at a school event. Her daughter Jada, who was in a coma for over five years, has since passed, but Elizabeth wanted to share her story.

"Although Jada is no longer with us, I guess I wanted to share my experiences and my love for my daughter because in a way, I can relate to other mothers' pain of having a child who has become incapable of caring for themselves—sometimes for years. If I didn't understand it before, I understand it now and I feel their pain.

For the five years before Jada passed, she lived in a hospice, and even though she did have a nurse, we visited her every day and saw to her daily needs, including hygiene. She was not able to do anything for herself and we did it for her, but it was very hard knowing that she could once do it all by herself.

As a result of what happened to my family as the result of Jada's hidden illness, one thing I wanted to reiterate to those who take it for granted, is that being surprised by having to deal with a disability when you weren't expecting it, can devastate a family, especially mothers.

As a mother of a child who could once do everything, I know that children don't necessarily have to be born with disabilities to still be considered disabled and it was one of the most hurtful and immobilizing experiences of my life.

One of the struggles I faced was accepting and admitting that my child was disabled, when one minute she was hanging out with her friends, helping out at home, playing with her sister and brother, being an outstanding student, and then everything changed. Jada was an awesome child and one of the best kids a parent could ever hope for, but we had no idea that her life would end so quickly, and that our lives would never be the same again.

"When it first happened and we found out about her brain tumor, it was incredibly difficult seeing her with tubes all over her head and body after surgery. I don't know from which area my pain came from most, from seeing her lying there like that, or from my own overwhelming grief about the whole situation.

It took months, which led to years, but we just had to take it day by day. However, I somehow I got through it and was able to breathe again, just like the powerfully moving poem "Footprints In The Sand," says. When you don't have the power or the strength to walk anymore, God carries you. It's a poem which I've always liked to read for comfort. I know that it was God who carried me through those difficult times, and I know He is still carrying me.

If it weren't for the love of God, my husband, my other children, and the prayers of my close friends and family, I don't know what I would have done. I know I wouldn't be fighting for some semblance of normalcy in my life again. I know that my family would have fallen apart and that I probably would have lost my mind.

All I know is I couldn't have made it on my own

and even to this day, I still need to draw on all their strength as the pain lessens little by little, bit by bit, as time slowly goes by."

Helga says that through the almost daily battles she faced in raising her son to adulthood, she has become a calmer, less combatant person—at least when she knows her children are safe and secure from hurt, harm and danger. But there was a time, when she would take the battles out of God's hands and try to take them on herself.

"I was once a fierce, rebellious young girl and teenager and even as an adult, was ready to floor anyone who got in my way. I guess it was because of my devastating childhood experience. In addition to the childhood abuse, I remember even as a child I used to be shut out by kids my age and I never really knew why, so I can understand what our children go through.

As a result, although I was friendly, I wouldn't let anyone get too close—and I still don't. I was distrustful of most people and I'd fight anything that moved if I had to. However, I am a changed person now since I had my children and since the Lord found me and I found Him. Since having Moses, I have learned to be more patient, less defiant, more trusting, more enduring and most importantly, I've learned to blame God less and love Him more, even as He taught me to love myself.

Now realize that through this whole thing, God

was teaching me and giving me the strength to lay down my earlier pain to become less self absorbed, less vengeful, although this was my armor, my protection from hurt when it came to certain people.

He wanted me to become more forgiving and more loving--characteristics that were always in me, but they were hidden deep inside. But I can now draw my strength and determination derived from these feelings, keeping me from reverting to my old destructive behavior and start looking forward to what's in front of me."

Like Helga, Debbie says that although she put on a stoic front for others, she was slowly losing her strength and no one knew it. She nearly lost her grip on her perception of life and no one knew she was fighting an inner battle.

"I nearly had a breakdown when I learned of Terrance's disability—I didn't know how to handle it, nor would I accept anyone's help in dealing with it. I always thought I had strict control over my life, however God quickly showed me that control is not at all what it's cracked up to be. Life doesn't have to be perfect for it to have value, nor do people.

I had worked very hard to earn my degrees, I secured a great position in my chosen profession, and I was used to dotting all my " i's" and crossing all my "t's." Terrance's physical and mental challenges really took the wind out of my sails, but I was able to recover from the pain—perhaps a bit faster than most, because I was determined to, and in a way, it helped ease the pain.

While I was recovering from the shock, I learned very quickly that I needed something stronger than myself to lean on. I never really had much of a relationship with God, but I guess, through this whole experience, He was taking hold of me and shaking me into reality—letting me know that I couldn't get through this without Him and now I wouldn't even try."

In contrast to my ignorance, Helga's defiance and Debbie's disillusion about perfection, Jennifer knew from experience what it was like to have a member of your family live with a disability. She grew up with a brother who became disabled in high school and she had a daughter born with physical and mental challenges.

"My brother was my hero. He was very smart and very handsome and after he became paralyzed playing high school football, he was very bitter. I saw how my mother handled it all. Although it hurt her very deeply, she approached the hardship with faith, love, tenderness, and forgiveness.

I guess that was what helped to prepare me for my own trauma of raising a child with a disability.

I too had been through a lot growing up. I lost a child from a miscarriage and a few years later, my daughter Nancy, was born with a number of physical and mental challenges, including Downs Syndrome, a chromosome disorder that is not hereditary. So we were more than a little surprised when this happened.

I am convinced however, that Nancy's disabilities stemmed from the time when my husband worked on a military base where there was nuclear dumping taking place, unknown to the people who lived there. By the time we moved and had Nancy, we realized we had been in the midst of it.

Over the years, accepting Nancy's disability has been quite a struggle, even today. I should be used to it, because of what happened to my brother, but that was different. Roger was able to speak, smile and take care of himself, where my daughter is not able to do any of those things. There used to be a time when I would just lay down and cry for my daughter and for what had become of my life. And although I don't understand why Nancy was born the way she was, over time my heart began to heal. I thank God He gave me the support I needed through my parents, my husband and my other children.

Yes, I was very angry at first, but I've since come to terms with the fact that even though my daughter has disabilities, she too has a purpose for being here and it was my responsibility to bring her into this world, to love her, to care for her and fight for her life. And although it doesn't seem possible because of all she's not able to do, I'm not giving up hope on Nancy and her possible recovery...the battle for her isn't over yet."

"Plan to win the battle, by seeking God both day and night, but never enter a war yourself, just trust God to win the fight..."

MOTHERHOOD

Motherhood, a job like no other
To whom every child is a special child
Not unlike those who are their mothers
Their special children are loved the same
At times she weeps, but covers the pain
What is a mother? It's hard to say
What we see is the inner fight to be whole,
As mothers love with all their heart and soul
No matter whom you meet in life,
There's nothing like the love of a mother
She's the one seeking the best for her child
No matter what crises she faces, all the while
God makes mothers tender, loving and strong
Soothing all pains, righting all wrongs
A wonder to all who observe them
Giving to all who allow them
A joy to all who have them,
Precious, a sparkling gem like no other
No need to take time to wonder, why
Like God who wants us to draw nigh,
There's just nothing like the love of a mother

Chapter Three
Mending Through Motherhood

Pour out your heart like water before the face of the Lord. Lift your hands toward Him For the life of your young children...Lamentations 2:19

All mothers are elected ladies, special women who come in all shapes, sizes, colors and cultures. Many mothers are married and others are single, some have children who can walk, talk, hop, skip, jump and think like other children their age, while others have children who are delayed in their development and can't do as many things as other children, but in both cases, nothing less than the best will do for our children.

There are times when we have all pursued (and probably are still pursuing) various ideals, visions and opportunities, which can enhance our quality of life and the lives of our children. This of course, includes their education, socialization, financial stability and spirituality.

So imagine the role and heart of a mother of a special needs child. In many cases, due to the tenaciousness of mothers (and most fathers), many of their dreams come to pass, but just as many times, they do not. Not necessarily because these mothers didn't try, but because they got discouraged from the insensitivity, inconsistency, inadequacy and inability found in the systems and relationships that were supposed to help their kids grow and blossom, rather than regress and stagnate.

For mothers like us who make the rearing of our children their ultimate priority, we don't take kindly to having our children disregarded...this is for any mother, but is especially the case for mothers with special needs children.

Even though our daily activities can sometimes be a little overwhelming at times, we still find inexpressible joy in gently, but sternly guiding, loving and nurturing our children, while continually praying for our young ones' healing and protection by the covering of God and His angels.

In essence, the majority of mothers of all children (not counting the unstable, dispassionate, unloving ones), are among the sweetest, most loving, kindest, smartest women around...but don't mess with us when it comes to the lives of our children or you'll have a whole different type of woman to deal with.

As shared before in the case of myself and Helga, married or single, with special needs kids or not, there is another side of us that we try to keep hidden from view. Those who've crossed the boundaries realize in short order that they've made

41

a dangerous, if not life-threatening mistake.

When it comes to the pain, strain and challenges mothers experience when raising their physically and/or mentally challenged child, they tend to become more than a little aggressive-- more like quarterbacks, pushing through to get to the finish line to achieve what we want—the total healing of our child. In many cases, we're going against the odds, but we're willing to take on the offensive line if we have to. As mothers of these children, we totally ignore the crowds of disbelieving doctors, family members, etc., until we get the desired results, tackling anyone who gets in our way.

When a loving mother with a special needs child sees an open door for the betterment of her child, she runs through it before it closes and loses the opportunity forever. Pushing through until we get what we need and want, is what we do best.

Like the story of the woman in the bible, who had been hemorrhaging for many years (Matthew 9:20-22). It doesn't say if she was a mother or not, but it's possible she may have been, at the very least, she was a woman with her own special needs--pushing and fighting for a different, more fulfilling life and did what she had to in order to get it.

Because of her determination and strength, she wouldn't let anything get in the way of what she saw was her healing—of whatever it was that was draining the life blood out of her. When she finally saw her open door for healing by touching the hem of Jesus' garment, she believed she would be healed and wouldn't take no for an answer and pushed her way through the detractors and obstacles, until that was exactly what took place.

Such boldness and determination of the hundreds of thousands of mothers with physically and mentally challenged children, is a characteristic they find within themselves, that many never even knew they had. I never thought of myself as such a woman—I was once shy and somewhat of a people pleaser. Believe me, I'm not that way any longer.

Since discovering Sierra's disability, I've become much more confrontational. I had become a woman whose purpose was now wrapped up in my child. I had become somewhat like a mother bear, protecting her cub—that's the way all elected ladies are when it comes to their children. We can be sweet as pie one moment, but fierce, unrelenting and even a bit frightening, when we have to be. Thankfully, we don't have to show that side of ourselves too often, just when necessary.

As a result of that characteristic I found in me, Sierra is very secure, intelligent and assertive and won't accept anyone telling her what she can or can't do. She may not be able to express it (yet), but I know she doesn't believe her future is limited in any way--just like we as her parents don't. She may not be able to walk or talk yet, but she's very feisty and communicates in her own unique way letting people know in no uncertain terms that she is not pleased with something—even with me!

I'm glad this doesn't happen too often. She does

this with me more than her father because with her he's a softie where she's concerned. As her parents we know when to nip her little screaming matches in the bud. We do, however, understand her need to express her feelings and individuality very clearly and we are kind of proud to see her be able to make attempts at doing so.

She has been blessed to have teachers who really care about her progress, for which I am extremely grateful. I'm always on the scene—sometimes unexpectedly, and they have come to know that I am very watchful of the education and care she receives at the public high school she is attending, and the elementary and middle schools she attended growing up.

I am happy to say that all the way through school, her teachers continue to show their professionalism and educational expertise with Sierra, challenging her to work at her optimal level and foremost, display the patience and loving care necessary to deal with our daughter.

Like most mothers, I don't want Sierra to miss out on anything, not even the latest fashions. (She is one of the most best dressed students at school). In fact, I'm told that other girls who are not in the special education program often ask about Sierra and admire her stylish outfits. As you can see, we don't even want her to miss out on high school teen jealousy!

We don't want her to miss out on enjoying her own style of music (she loves contemporary gospel, old school R&B, and a little rap (the clean kind)! We also don't want her to miss out on learning about computers (she participates in her school's educational programs for developmentally delayed children). Anything that's going to help her growth and development into a typically (or atypically) advanced teenager and young adult we want her to have a part in it, if possible. (Alright, I am kind of glad she isn't interested in what most teenagers her age are today—although she does have a crush on Helga's son).

I bring up holiday seasons, because as Sierra's mother, at first, that was a particularly difficult time for me. My childhood memories are especially great and I want to ensure that Sierra had a boat load of childhood memories too. As I shared earlier when she was a toddler through her early teen years, she didn't really understand what Christmas was all about, what to get excited about or what to do. She had no interest if she received presents or not.

I'm happy to say that she fully understands it now and tears the wrapping off her many presents, as fast as we give them to her.

As she gets older and is now a young adult, we are moving into another phase of Sierra's life, like any teen, she likes getting new clothes, likes her privacy and is learning to spend money (through her schools community based instruction program). Also, like any teenage girl, she likes handling money and going shopping (although she's just starting to get an idea of what to do with it and what to spend it on). She is even starting to notice boys, but although wary and nervous, I look forward to sharing this new chapter in her life and development with her, by guiding her (and her father) through it. It's all part of our roles as mothers, and what we look forward to doing for the lives, growth and future of our children.

I now understood where my mother was coming from when she did anything she had to do in her power for the love and lives of her children. If that meant working two jobs, getting little rest, being overly protective, and even taking on the neighborhood bullies, she was ready to do it. I fondly remember her coming out to the playground in her robe and slippers once, to make sure that a bully that tried to harass us and beat on us, never thought to do that again. In fact, she scared them so much, we later became friends.

My mother was and is still an incredible woman, despite having a few unique qualities as do all of us, she was one the hardest working, sweetest women I knew growing up. Now retired, I can see how much she believed in us and wanted to serve as a role model for us. It worked too, because through faith, love and hard work, she showed us how we could have whatever we wanted, and we all strived to get it.

She showed us how to never give up, to keep at something until we saw the manifestation of what we wanted, come to pass—even if we couldn't see the fruits of our labor yet and that took much more time than we would have liked. Now that's true faith. As a result, I am able to wait as patiently as possible for what I believe will be Sierra's ability to do just about everything anyone else can do—and I look forward to its manifestation. It's what my mother did, despite life's challenges.

My mother and my father divorced when I was about 10 and up until then, I saw her stand and withstand some very painful moments with my dad. Even so, she continued to express her love for her eight children by making sure we had a warm, comfortable, loving and safe haven.

Many years later after most of us have married and now live elsewhere it's always good to come home. She worked very hard, but mental and physical abuse she endured from the many years married to my father, took its toll on her.

However, due to her innate strength and our consistent prayers, she is working through all of that. Now nearly 80 years-old, she still looks great, and trying to enjoy the rest of her life while still looking out for the best interest of her grown children and grand kids. She is still the protective mother hen she always was, and I guess she always will be. Here she shares some of her story.

"I'm a product of the Caribbean culture which said the man had all the say in the house and could do anything he wanted with no say from his wife or anyone else and you stayed married whether you wanted to or not.

I married when I was 16 and back then, marriages were arranged for money and my family had wealth. After beginning to have my children, I saw their father less and less, although he was still my husband, I never knew where he was half the time—but he was home enough to give me eight children—all of which I loved dearly.

I was married for 22 years and after my divorce as the result of a physically, emotionally and mentally abusive marriage, I, put all my love and attention into raising my children, half of which were still very young. Next to my mother, my children were my only family and I did whatever I could for them. It wasn't easy back then, but we made due and my life wasn't any different from many of the women of that time. I did what I could with what I had, worked hard and just tried to make sure that my children had what they needed and were as happy as I could help make them, and I believe they were—that's what mothers do."

Losing Something to Gain Something

It wasn't until I became an adult that I realized just how much my mother sacrificed in her own personal life to give us the relatively carefree lives we had as children. I know now how much we took this for granted. At least the younger set of four did, of which I was one, who experienced less of the household chaos than the older four children.

I can now reflect on those times and see that my mother was also a chosen woman, like so many other mothers out there—then and now. As a result, I've learned what real strength in a woman is like and what married life should and should not be like. These were key lessons which I learned from her and have never forgotten.

To me, my mother exhibited much strength and determination and was filled with many gifts and talents, which unfortunately, she never really got the chance to explore. I believe I love music today because of my mother, who would sing and play hymns and songs to us that she learned growing up on the small Caribbean island of Monserrat, West Indies.

My younger brothers and sisters and I would gather around in her bedroom in the Harlem projects we grew up in, and listen to her sing and play songs from an acoustic guitar she owned. As a result, there were quite a few of us in the family with a penchant for music and who had talent in that area, because of the talent she passed on to us.

If she ever had any dreams of her own, she never really talked about them—it just seemed that she focused mostly on us. We had wonderful holiday celebrations, always had new clothes for Easter and new toys for Christmas (back then they had layaway!), she even saved her pennies to buy us a piano and paid for piano lessons, which my younger sister and I never appreciated and stopped taking them--a decision I regret to this day.

After a shooting outside our first floor apartment door, she saved money to take us out of the projects a year or so later. We moved into a beautiful 18-room white stucco house in Mount Vernon, New York, which she purchased for little or nothing. The house was located in what is still a relatively affluent suburb of Westchester County.

Although at the time the price was a little steep for my mom, as a result of her vision, business savvy and expensive tastes, the value of that house has increased to more than 20 times what she paid for it and it's now worth a pretty penny in New York real estate. Her goal was and still is, to pass the home down through the generations, so that her children and grandchildren will always have a safe place to which to come home and wealth to divide, if ever needed.

My mother fought hard for all her children and I am indebted to her for everything she taught me and for my happy childhood memories, and I hope to be as good a mother to Sierra as she was to all of us.

Another mother who had a profound affect on me as a child and even as a grown woman today—is my mother-in-law, Mary Stanley. I also call her mom and she was and still is one of the sweetest women I know, but could be a pistol when necessary. Anyone who knew her loved her, but they also knew not to mess with her.

I've known Mom Stanley since I was a little girl having grown up with her children in the same apartment building. It was from her that I learned how to fight for and sustain a loving marital relationship—even when it was sometimes difficult.

Always someone to whom I could turn to when there were issues in my 20 plus years of marriage to her son that needed sorting through, Mom Stanley was an objective listener and was full of wisdom and sensitivity about love and life. If she had any personal aspirations, she also never talked about it and always seemed quite content just caring for her family. When so many of my friends have issues with their mothers-in-law, it's great to know that I have one who, in addition to my biological mom, I could always turn to, although for different reasons.

While my own mother loved and prayed constantly for my physically and mentally challenged daughter Sierra, she really had had no experience with children like these so she couldn't really relate. This is in contrast to my mother-in-law, who worked with special needs kids as part of her job as a para-professional teacher, for over 30 years. As a result, Mom Stanley was able to relate to Sierra differently and understands her in a way that sometimes my own mother doesn't, although I know my mother loves Sierra.

"I pray every night for God's protection over my granddaughter, Sierra, other children with special needs and their mothers, and my heart goes out to them. I've always loved children and loved my job working with elementary school kids in the New York City public school system.

51

Some of the children with whom I worked were mentally challenged, but I treated all the children in the same way—equally loving and kind, yet stern when necessary, trying to be like a mother to them when they were in my classroom. I guess in a way, that was God also getting me ready for what was ahead, the birth of my granddaughter, Sierra.

I saw what the mothers of these children were going through and I tried to do what I could to ease their pain--at least when their children were in school. Some of these children came from abusive households, where their parents didn't know how to handle them and these were not necessarily just the children with special needs.

Although I've always treated my school kids with love and respect, when Sierra was born, I was even more adamant about how inclusive and friendly the children were to each other, because I wanted kids around Sierra to be the same.

I also tried to ensure wherever I could, that no adult took advantage of any child in my care—not even by their own parents. With the way the world is today, that is an area for which I pray especially hard, because children like Sierra are so vulnerable—not being able to talk, walk or communicate—I hate to see or hear about any of them being hurt. So I try to do what I can, to make sure things like that don't happen, at least where it is in my control. I have little or no tolerance for those who harm children—any child--especially those with special needs.

Here it is so many years later, I can see what my two mothers were trying teach me in their own individual way—not even realizing they were doing so. In my birth mother, I saw the struggle, strength, fight, determination and willpower buffeted by motherly love that you had to have to make life better for your children, despite not having their dad around. Sadly, this is a situation that too many women face today.

In watching Mom Stanley and her household in which I'm glad my husband grew up, I saw a picture of what I always believed a two-parent household was supposed to be—warm, loving, playful, with boundaries set when and where necessary.

I'm happy to say that my husband and I have also been able to provide our daughter with a warm, loving home. Sierra was always a pretty little girl (if I do say so myself!) and has grown into an even prettier young woman. Actually she looks more like her father (with very little of me thrown in), but much of her outgoing personality comes from me.

For the most part, just like her mom, she's always happy curious, loves to laugh, loves music and singing (she can't really talk yet, but she knows how to hum a tune really well)! She also loves to cook like her mom, (which equates to making her own peanut butter and jelly sandwiches and making popcorn in the microwave...with supervision). Her personality, her talents, her likes and dislikes are very much like mine.

But when it comes to her relationship with her father, she is daddy's little darling and I had to get used to it. When her Dad is around, I don't exist and that used to bother me that the two of them were so close, but I finally came to a point where I was happy about their relationship. There are so many fathers who walk away from children like ours, and I'm glad to see that these two people could not be any more attached. Although Sierra cannot talk, she has her own way special way of communicating with her dad that I love to observe.

Her dad is very playful and acts silly with her and he's the one she calls when she wants to play. He let's her beat him up, (which I won't let her do to me, because she's got a powerful punch). However, I'm the one she calls when she wants to eat, turn on her stereo and do the regular things-- basically everything else, but I'm glad that I have a daughter who knows that I'm always there for her— whether she can communicate that in words or not.

Being a good mother is full of love and personal sacrifices and there's nothing more valuable than working to secure the best lives for our children. Sometimes that includes sacrificing individual hopes and dreams, but as shared earlier, most of us come out that much better because of that sacrifice. And just like every mother out there can attest, by coming through the fire, we have become the kind of women and mothers we are today and for me, that's a good thing.

Having gone through a difficult childhood and

becoming the mother of three, when it came to raising her two daughters and her son, Helga was adamant that they did not endure the same hardships that she did as a child, so as a mother she sacrificed much to gain even more.

"I wanted to see my children have the life that I never really had. I wanted them to have a life full of love, fun, expectancy, joy and safety. I wanted them to know that nothing could harm them, because their parents wouldn't let that happen. I especially love that my two daughters have grown into intelligent, talented, determined and independent individuals, careful not to let anyone take advantage of them—something I taught them at an early age.

I love the fact that my oldest daughter, Melony, has grown into such a financially savvy young woman, who in her mid twenties is already becoming a success at investing and preparing for her financial future. She is also a very giving young lady and would do anything for her family, especially her brother and others in need, which is another thing about her of which I am very proud..

My other teenaged daughter Brittany, is equally as loving to her brother and highly intelligent and talented. With the intention of becoming a fashion designer, she already has her own label and I believe is going to take the fashion world by storm. I'd like to think I had something to do with my daughters' intelligence, talent and drive, because they have a lot of me in them.

Next to my daughters, my son is light of my life. Despite him being born with mental and physical challenges, I am extremely grateful that God is allowing his continued growth to negate what doctors had predicted about him.

Moses continues to make positive strides every day and is doing many of the things they thought he would never do, beating many of the odds. His continued development makes me very happy and very proud of his on-going physical and mental growth and his own fight to become as whole as possible.

I used to wonder if I was a good mother to any of them. I can only smile now as I look back and honestly and confidently say to myself and even the world that yes I was and I am still, a good mother!"

Speaking of beating all the odds as a mother, no one expected Kate, having been born with cerebral palsy to ever get married, much less give birth to perfectly a normal, physically and mentally able son.

"I consider him to be the best thing that ever happened to me. My son has always been remarkably bright from day one and he was very loving and protective as a young boy, while he was also very independent, supportive and patient.

Actually, in a lot of ways he taught me to have a lot more patience with people. If he ever thought of

*having a mother with a disability as being a
negative thing, he never expressed it to me. He was
always very playful, loving and very protective of
me.*

*He was a wonderful child, although I didn't
know which one of us would survive his puberty, but
we did. And today, he has grown into a wonderful
adult, with a family of his own. He has always been
a true blessing to me and I thank God for him."*

I can't even imagine the pain in which Elizabeth
has had to suffer through, but it's another example
of how strong God has had to make us as mothers—
some even more than others.

*It's been a few years now, and I've come to
some terms with it what happened to Jada, but there
was a time early in the experience, where I hated
myself as a mother. I would ask myself, "How could
you not have noticed there was something wrong?
What kind of a mother are you?" Of course, there
was nothing wrong with my mothering or me, it was
just part of my life's assignment and I soon learned
later, part of my ministry. However, after God
called Jada home earlier than any of us would have
expected, the questions really began and my anger
grew.*

*When she first went into a coma David refused
to let either of us give up hope or lose our faith. I
guess he was trying to help me especially, because I
was ready to give up.*

But Dave wouldn't let me. He kept praying and believing that she would someday, miraculously come out of the coma. In the meantime, I had to keep going, even though it was in a numb state.

My challenge has been to love my other children and my husband back to wholeness and keep them from giving up hope on themselves, on their futures and on life. At first, our son, who used to be such a good student, was ignoring his school work and his grades continued to slip. He was afraid that if he worked as hard as his sister Jada did, the same thing would happen to him. Through some counseling, he's now back on track as a tribute to his sister, but it took a while.

It took a while for all of us. I no longer hate God, although I admit, there was a time I did. Once God was my whole life, next my children, then I turned my back on him for a short time and even my children, after Jada's passing. But now I'm thankful that He's been there for me whether I wanted Him to be or not.

I now know that He was holding me, my husband and our other children, up and carrying us, and loving us when we could no longer do so ourselves. It was my time of weakness and emptiness as a mother and as a wife, but God knew it and filled in the cavernous gap with love, giving me back my needed strength so we all could go on— in peace and surrender.

As you can see from this sampling of

motherhood, the various experiences, emotions, memories both good and bad, the joys of being a mother, whether or not you have a special needs child, runs the gamut.

But as challenging as being a mother is to most, and the fact that it's more often than not, a very difficult road to travel, God gave mothers of special needs children the heart, strength and drive to deal with it all. We had to learn to manage our challenge like no other mother could, to be there for our children and help our kids have somewhat of a life. Just like any mother, we should be proud of the fact that God made us strong enough to handle the various trials that come our way, because now we know we can handle anything.

"A mother's light of love is like a beacon, shining from far away, but close enough to lead you home. When alone, lonely or lost, a true mother will be there, no matter what the cost."

GIRL INTERRUPTED

It all came so unexpectedly
Something I'd prayed would never be
But the path I had chosen, was somehow not God's
Now I can only draw on Him, to beat the odds
My life totally changed for ever more
I still have no idea of what is in store
This new challenge, now anchors my life
My purpose revealed through the pain of it all
Helped me reach deep inside to discover my call
Thinking myself, as a girl interrupted
Realizing my life with no faith was pre-empted
Whatever God's plan was first misunderstood
But for now I see, it was for the greater good
Looking ahead and forgetting what was
'Cause no one could fill my life,
The way my special child does

Chapter Four
Girl Interrupted

"Moreover, whom He predestined, these He also called; whom He called, these He also justified, and whom He justified, these He also glorified."
Romans 8:30

L ike everyone else, I've had some rough patches in my life, but I've always been able to get past them relatively quickly and relatively unscathed. At first I thought it was all because of my winning personality and how talented and smart I was--was I ever wrong!

It wasn't too long before I realized that those components had nothing to do with the success I had been enjoying up to that point in my life. It had much more to do with my misunderstanding the blessings, guidance, covering and calling God had on my life.

At one time or another, when we were young girls, we all have dreamed and aspired to have successful and exciting careers. I dreamed of becoming a successful and wealthy, corporate executive, singer (not necessarily famous), reporter, writer, as well as a wife and mother. And I am happy to say that I have been blessed for the most part, to have experienced most, if not all of those things at different phases of my life—some even simultaneously.

I was always a very career-oriented person. I had always dreamed of becoming a well-respected and renowned journalist like Barbara Walters, or TV news producer like Mary Richards on The Mary Tyler Moore Show. Actually, the person who really inspired me to become a journalist was Geraldo Rivera, who was a young, upwardly mobile Hispanic television journalist when I was first introduced to him when he spoke at my sixth grade graduation. Then Melba Tolliver, an African American television reporter in New York, spoke at my middle school graduation and I was hooked!

Although I didn't become a television journalist or producer, I did, however, become a newspaper journalist and surprisingly, found out that wasn't exactly my style either. My love for writing and my own creative need for expression, eventually led to a successful, award-winning career in public relations and marketing.

I was traveling internationally, working with many major multinational companies, organizations and celebrities in the television, film, sports, literary and music industries—basically, all my childhood career dreams wrapped up in one.

What I didn't know then, was that I was

supposed to experience all those challenging and character building life episodes, so I would be ready for what was ahead of me. Like I said earlier, having my daughter took all that I thought was meaningful away and it was then that I had to fall back on my faith in God, and found what was really meaningful. But at the time, I thought everything for which I'd worked so hard, was over.

God had interrupted the path of my former life, for which at first I thoroughly resented Him, but now realize that He did it to help me get to the stage I needed to be, a stage in my life which was going to take a little time to develop. This was obviously a level to which I needed to grow, before time ran out.

It was at that time when I truly began to seek a relationship with God. This search helped me search deep inside myself and fully connect with the strength lying dormant in me.

It was the birth of my now young adult daughter, Sierra, which led me back to God for answers. I began praying more, attending church more, stepping into new, challenging territories in faith and believing for future miracles for my daughter's life, as well my own.

I never really paid much attention to my spirituality, although I was raised to believe in God. We went to church sometimes when I was a little girl, but it was mostly on Easter and Christmas. I now know that God has been guiding me all this time to help me look past my early self-centeredness (which I didn't know I was), to opening up to include other lives in the world surrounding me. His goal was to turn me into the person I am now, both personally and professionally—and I can now thank him for His interruption with joy and expectation for what the future holds.

Many other mothers' lives have been interrupted by the life changing occurrence of having a special needs child, and have emerged more confident, more powerful, more considerate, more loving and even more excited about life, than even they thought they could ever be. The following are some other examples to which you might be able to relate.

"Growing up, I had always wanted to be a singer. When I turned 15, I was asked to join a very popular band in Savannah, where I sang lead. After being told by the audiences that I was a very good singer, I worked my way towards making a name for myself in the music industry. It was something that I believed I could do successfully and for which I had a gift, and worked diligently to see that dream come to pass.

I felt great when I was on stage, it was exciting, and made me feel confident about who I was and what I could do. At the time, this was something I only felt when I was on stage performing. That was a happy time for me, but unfortunately one of the band members was killed, the band broke up and never reunited.

Not long after that, I got married and started to have children, which took priority in my life, especially when I had Moses. I knew then that things regarding my singing career would change. So I put my music career on hold for a while, knowing that my life would never be the same again.

One of the biggest struggles that I faced at this juncture of my life was learning how to let go of my dream, as badly as I wanted to see it happen. I had to learn how to put my life and career on hold for the sake of my children, especially my son. It wasn't an easy decision, but I loved my son deeply and knew that I had no choice—at least not at the time. I certainly wasn't going to take the route that his doctors recommended, which was to give him up. Can you believe that is what the doctors suggested that I do? They wanted me to just walk away from him and there was no way I was going to do that.

What I soon realized was sometimes we are faced with situations that are extremely unpleasant, painful and event distasteful, but they can also be a turning point in your life. I understood that it wasn't so much about my life anymore, it was about Moses and my other children, and as a result, I began to grow up—really fast.

Giving Over Getting, Heals Pain

What I began to see was that sometimes in life it's not so much about what we want, but what God may have placed us here to do. I realize now, that my experience with raising Moses was part of my purpose, and also to help others in the same situation realize it all as a blessing. Although many mothers like me may think of having a child with physical and mental disabilities as a punishment, it really isn't. It's more of a growth experience, both for you and your child.

At first, I struggled with those feelings myself, because many aspects of my life growing up was filled with so much unhappiness and I thought getting married and having children would ease some of that pain.

Now here I was, again dealing with a trauma I wouldn't wish on anyone, but which had strangely become a staple and an anchor in my life. Although he was sometimes difficult to care for, Moses has always been deeply loved by his whole family, especially me. He is a very affectionate young man and I thank God every day for allowing Moses to be a part of our lives—both my immediate and extended family-- because it has helped us all to grow in the areas in which we all needed to grow.

Although I wanted to be in the music and entertainment business when I was younger, from what little I experienced of it, it was a dangerous place to be as a vulnerable young girl and I believe that God spared me from all the harmful possibilities that I may have faced. Because I was young and ambitious I could have made some unwise choices, but God interrupted my life with a child like Moses.

I know for a fact when I look back on my life, I was facing a fork in the road, one that had I not had Moses, it would have changed my life—negatively.

He knew that if I had not had a child like Moses, I wouldn't be walking in my destiny now. A destiny for which I am now wiser and more prepared for God's plans for me in this area, and as a result, I am more prepared to go after my dreams and see them all manifest, even though many of them have not only grown, but changed.

I so thank God so much for interrupting my life when he did. I realize now that he not only did it for me, and my best interests, but I believe in the best interest of my family and other families I haven't even met yet!"

Having your life interrupted by unplanned, unexpected and uncontrollable circumstances is something no one wants to experience, but when you're a stickler for detail, order and being in control, situations like having a child with disabilities, could turn someone's life absolutely upside down. That's exactly what happened to Debbie.

"My biggest struggle with all this was that I was a planner-- always putting things in order, believing

that being organized and thinking things through towards the future, ensured that nothing unexpected could happen. That's not at all how it turned out.

Needless to say, having a son born with special needs, really got in the way of my plans for my future, but I'm also a new person, more caring, compassionate, and even more focused because of it.

I wanted to be an architect, designing skyscrapers, office buildings, shopping complexes, etc., and the thought of it all was very exciting to me. I had gotten a pretty good start too, working with one of the top firms in Chicago.

I got married soon after starting as an apprentice with the firm on my way to becoming a full fledged associate. After a few years and a couple promotions, I got pregnant. Terrance was our first child and we soon found out after he was born, that he would be developmentally delayed.

It took a while to sink in, and I did what I could to go on trying to make whatever adjustments I needed to make. I kept working at an optimal level at my job, to keep the pace I once kept, almost ignoring my son.

Knowing how intense and exacting working as an architect was, as well as parenting a son with a disability who couldn't do anything for himself, it was at this time that I realized that having a big career was not what I needed at this time. I needed to be home to take care of my son, which I soon realized, was much more important to me than any job could be. So like so many mothers in this predicament do if they're able to, I stayed at home and focused my son.

I focused my time and energy towards my family, which at first I did a bit reluctantly. Like I explained, putting things in order was very important to me, especially financial stability, and our family suffered tremendously when I left my job.

Not exactly to my liking, the course of my career and life was interrupted, and if it had not been for the depth of my love for my family, I would have never known that my life was on a path of destruction anyway. I was losing my husband and didn't know it. During this time, I had become distant and unapproachable, lashing out at him for no reason.

With God's help, we were able to get past a potentially heartbreaking time for all of us. We have now returned to family and financial stability and I can breathe a little easier.

I am now a consulting architect with the flexibility to attend to my son's needs. The thoughts of the trauma intrinsic to the possibilities of the unexpected and unplanned, does not scare me as it once did. My experience with the unexpected and unplanned, is now turning out to be the impetus for my walk of faith, something I didn't realize I so desperately needed.

I never thought I'd say this, but truthfully, I've never been happier.

Fortunately, her innate love for children helped Elizabeth cope with her own life defining moment, which came as a total surprise. Jada, her first child, was born without a disability of any kind, and was being diagnosed years later with a brain tumor, just before graduating from high school. This of course, was a life interrupting, very traumatic and frightening position to be in.

"It was a crippling experience for me, and it just about killed me. My life was going so well! I had a great husband, three wonderful kids whom I adored and was looking forward to going back to school for another master's degree. I keep looking back at how wonderful it had been—almost from day one. But life is different now.

I had earned a post graduate degree in Science and Early Childhood Education and I have always loved to work with children-- holding and playing with babies. I married soon after receiving my degree and looked forward to building a life together with my new husband, who I actually met at college.

I began working at an elementary school near where I lived and loved working with the children. I was able to help them to develop, imagine, and explore the world of possibilities that lay ahead of them, through reading, writing and mathematics.

As an early education teacher, I had the opportunity to work with a few children with mild special needs and found it very rewarding to see how with attention and patience, over time, they would learn what the other children were learning. It was a wonderful experience and I looked forward to doing more of it.

After a couple years, I found I was pregnant and my first child was born, a beautiful baby girl, named Jada. Although Jada was not exactly planned, I didn't mind having my goals blocked at the moment, as she was the best thing that ever happened to us. As a young couple, it was a very happy time in our lives, but who would have thought that happiness would turn to sorrow one day, and that our lives would seemingly forever be put on hold.

I continued to work as a special education teacher for a few years after the birth of Jada, but not long after that our son Brian was born and then our youngest daughter, Samantha and my husband and I decided it was best for the family if I remained at home to care for the kids.

Although I had a master's degree in a field that I loved and enjoyed doing, I had no problem with the fact that I was home being a mother and wife and raising our children...in fact I received immeasurable joy in it. I saw my children grow into brilliant (although I might be a little biased), hard working, out-going and respectful kids and we were both very proud of them.

Our oldest daughter Jada was an honor student and leader throughout high school and was even picked to be the valedictorian of her senior class.

Jada was a month or so away from graduation, when she passed out giving a speech at her school. We found out that she had a malignant tumor on the stem of her brain and from that point on, life was never the same—for any of us.

The whole thing took a part of my heart that I know will never be replaced...but after a period of time—a very, very, very long time, I learned to somehow get past it all and started moving on. Just before we learned of her tumor, I was in my late 30's and was busily preparing for her graduation. I was working on last minute details for the surprise graduation trip with the whole family to Hawaii (a place she'd always wanted to visit) when we got the news. After that, it seemed as if time had stopped.

There is nothing more painful than learning of your child's unexpected disability and possible death, which I know personally, can make you doubt yourself and God.

It seemed like my husband and I couldn't stop crying; our other children did not understand why this happened to their older sister, as neither did we. We were at the hospital day and night and we had never prayed so hard in our lives. However, she is now with the Lord and in some ways, it is almost a burden lifted from me.

We prayed almost incessantly while she laid in that coma and I tried so hard to prepare myself and my family for the possibility that she may never come out of it. Those conversations even caused some friction between me and my husband, because he refused to believe that possibility. But he eventually had to accept God's will, as did I, trust that God knew best and pick up the pieces of our lives where we could and move on.

I don't know exactly why God allowed this to happen, but if my experience of being a mother to a child who once was able to do everything, who then went to being able to do nothing, and who then had a child taken from us, perhaps I can help ease someone else's burden going through the same thing.

My family and I are slowly recuperating from our loss and have been shocked into the realization that God never said life was fair, but that we would, in fact, get through our challenges.

I see the glimmer of light coming through the darkness, as I watch my other children grow and I enjoy every moment with them and helping other mothers through difficult circumstances—and because of this, the pain gets easier, and my life gets fuller.

Kate faced her own defining moment being born with physical challenges from a different perspective—one of lightheartedness, strength, purpose and determination.

"I believe that God has a sense of humor and he had to think long and hard to create me. Although some may consider my being born with cerebral palsy a negative thing, I believe in many ways it

was definitely more positive and don't consider my condition to be an interruption, but an opportunity.

It has been an opportunity to change people's perception of the physically and mentally challenged. Although I am not mentally challenged, I am physically challenged and I believe that my being here was not an accident.

Not only did God give me all the tools I needed to do what I had to do to improve the options for the disability community locally and nationally, he also gave me vision and the ability to see things from perspectives that not everyone can see.

In addition, my sense of humor allows me not to get bitter at the reception of others, but to retain my dignity and uniqueness. It helps me to stay proud of myself and what I have accomplished in life, despite my physical challenges.

I can't say that is has been easy, but I can say because of those close to me, the pain has been buffeted by love. For the most part, it has been full of joy and a daily educational experience for me and others sharing my view of life. It has also been challenging, yet inspiring and I know that God's decision to put me here at this time was the right time to make a significant difference for the growing disability community.

I have an ability to see humor in almost everything. I tend to see the good in everyone, have a desire to learn something every day, and the determination to serve as an advocate for this community. No, my being born with cerebral palsy has not interrupted my life in fact, it has enriched it—but through my life, it has interrupted the lives of others and opened up their eyes to what's needed, which is my express purpose for being here."

"When life interrupts your dreams and your plans, don't ask why. Turn your face to the heavens, stand on the rock of salvation and keep your head to the sky."

CHOSEN MEN FOR CHOSEN WOMEN

God's Word says man should not be alone
So He created Eve from Adam's rib bone
Two people meant to meet, their hearts start to
flutter
A passion begins, a feeling of wonder
The sweet words of love soon to be spoken
A real bond is formed, not meant to be broken
Then from life harsh realities hit
Tearing both your hearts to bits
Tossing you both to and fro
Not knowing what to do, where to go
The pain of it all throws you for a loop
Yet your love for each other gives you strength to
recoup
For a chosen woman, finding your chosen man is
not something that can be planned, it has to just
happen. For a chosen woman who God has
assigned to do more
Only a chosen man could understand and support
The chaos life brought sending most away
Yet like God's chosen woman, he's elected to stay
Somewhere out of time, a real love, a new joy arose
And only women who choose to, can recognize
those
I'm sorry that for you, it may not yet be
But I know this is the man God has chosen for me

Chapter Five
Chosen Men For Chosen Women

"Therefore a man shall leave his father and mother and be joined to his wife and they shall become one flesh." Genesis 3:24

For a chosen woman, finding your a chosen man is not something that can be planned, it has to just happen. Finding a mate or prospective husband with whom you synchronize, with whom there is positive energy, a man who not only covers you, but protects you, understands you and takes care of you—in good times and bad, is not an easy thing to do.

I believe that kind of union has to be ordained and predestined by God—it's not happenstance, nor is it an overnight discovery. Just like in the case of Mary, the mother of Jesus. Engaged to Joseph, she had no idea she would carry and birth the son of God, but was chosen to do so.

Just as her husband Joseph was chosen for her, by God. Joseph had to be one special man, because although he did not understand what was happening and could have caused shame to Mary by sharing that the baby she was carrying was not his, he listened with his heart through a dream.

In this dream, he is told by an angel not to be afraid to take Mary into his home as his wife and to take care of her, the baby and raise him as his own. Not even questioning it, Joseph listened and opened his heart—something that only a few special men today are willing to do, and followed the words of the angel.

To find a man like Joseph or any chosen man by God, takes time, sometimes more time than many of us are willing to wait. Unfortunately, today women of all ages are looking through rose colored glasses and have been searching for a loving relationship— of any kind. Looking through rose colored glasses is not necessarily a bad thing, but searching for a loving relationship of any kind can do us more harm than good.

As a result, many women sometimes don't take the necessary length of time to find out if personalities, characteristics, likes and dislikes, visions and spiritual faith are compatible. It may not be that all aspects are compatible, but there should be more compatibilities than less.

These are all keys to finding their chosen man. That is not to say that the two have to be matched in every way, there will be differences, of course, but differences that fill the voids in each other's emptiness—not add to them.

I am certainly no expert, but I have noticed that in many cases, when women rush into relationships before God is ready for a relationship to take place, disastrous things seem to happen. These are things that not only hurt the woman, but the children that may result from the union. Someone they want to believe is prince charming, actually turns out to be a frog—bailing out on them in critical times.

If you think this happens with women whose children don't have any mental and physical challenges, can you imagine how often it happens with women who do have special needs children? Unfortunately, that happens more often than not, and the additional stress is more overwhelming and painful than many can take.

That's not to say that there aren't men who support their wives and children in these emotionally taxing situations, because there are. However, in these cases, I believe these men were specifically chosen by God to be husbands, mates, providers and protectors of these chosen women and their children, and to be there for them through thick and thin.

I am truly blessed to be able to say that my husband and I have experienced the case of being "chosen" for each other. Although in many instances we are as different as night is from day and there have been many thin days as opposed to thick, we're very much alike in many ways. We both have similar upbringings, similar characteristics, and similar goals (for the most part)—even though we sometimes go about achieving them in different ways.

Steven and I were childhood buddies, and grew up together in the same building in New York. Both our parents were alike in that they worked diligently and were adamant about keeping their children off the streets and away from dangerous influences. The only difference was that he grew up in a two-parent household and I grew up in a single-parent household.

It was those traits that probably attracted me to him and his family in the first place. My father rarely came around, except on holidays and birthdays when we would have great gatherings at our house (my mom was such a great cook). However, I always saw my husband's family together – going to church, grocery shopping, going fishing, taking trips to the south, where his parents grew up and just having a great time together. They even seemed to enjoy just hanging out together quietly at home.

Mom and Dad Stanley were very friendly, but strict parents, not allowing their two sons Walter, Steven and their daughter, Jeanine to hang out in the streets like many of the other parents. They had to be inside the house by a certain time, which was usually before it got dark, just like we did. So we kept out of the kind of trouble that many of the other kids in the neighborhood were getting into.

Steven and I "courted" for a few months when I was almost 15, and I fondly remember his carrying my books home from school and talking to me outside our kitchen window (we weren't allowed to have company when mom wasn't home—especially boys!) of our first floor apartment. He did this even in the dead cold of winter, risking frost bite to the fear of this mother. He would talk to me as I prepared dinner for our family while my mother and older sisters were at work, and teased me about how many different ways I could make chicken—which was a lot. Chicken was just about all we ate, when my mother was saving for our new house. We laughed a lot back then and still do.

Then for some reason one day, he just stopped speaking to me...I was very hurt for a while, and never understood why, but I was too busy with maintaining my grades to think about it much. Not long after that, my family moved to the suburbs, I graduated from high school, I heard that Steven had joined the army and I had not seen nor heard from him until after I graduated from college.

Then, seven years later, a few days after graduating from college I visited my old neighborhood and a friend of mine who lived around the corner from where my family used to live. I heard a quiet voice say me, "Go around the corner to see if you see anyone you grew up with, and lo and behold, who do I run into, but Steven! We talked, went to the movies (our first real date) and have been together ever since—26 years (22 of them married) later. Am I giving away my age? I'm not as old as that sounds!

It wasn't until after we'd been married for over 10 years, that Steven revealed to me that my mother had told him to stay away from me when we were younger, because I was getting distracted from my school work, and she wanted to make sure I didn't get off track. That was the reason he didn't talk to me anymore when we were sophomores in high school and he never told me the reason why back then, he just obeyed. I respected and loved him even more when he told me that (although I was furious with my mother)!

As different as we are, my husband and I still find ways to connect on levels some of our family and friends don't understand, but God says to lean not to our own understanding. He's been there for me and our daughter when we needed him most, he still makes me laugh after more than 20 years of marriage; we have fun together and he's a very caring and attentive father to Sierra. It's been a whirlwind of a ride and although we've had our share of blustery storms over the years, God and our love for each other, has kept us from being blown in separate ways.

I'm sure there are many other women out there who can attest to their own "chosen man," but here are some opinions and examples of love experiences my friends have shared on this topic. Let's begin with Elizabeth.

Chosen Men, Love for a Lifetime or Love as Our Lifeline

"Once you have made a choice for your mate, it should be a lifetime choice. I believe my husband has also been chosen for me in every way, but particularly spiritually. We met in college and have always had so much in common. Although it has been a struggle for both of us at times, we took our marriage vows seriously and planned to keep those vows.

When you experience something as painful as what we've experienced as a result of our daughter's tragic situation, the pain of it all sometimes helps to make the marriage stronger; it brings you closer together.

You may not be able to see it at first, but after a while if you continue to endure these devastating times of life where you can't see it, then you do come out on the other side. If there was true love and a real bond before the storm hit, you do come out with a more loving marriage, where you comfort each other and draw from each others' strength. You realize the other blessings of God that surround you daily and never take anything else for granted.

We can't all just drop out of a relationship at the first signs of trouble. I've found that if a couple works at facing their problems together and not give up on the love that brought them together, it makes them both stronger emotionally and spiritually.

83

I'm not saying that this always works, but I found that in my marriage when things were the hardest for us—particularly around the time of Jada's coma when there was a lot of friction and ugly words spoken, we had to rely on those early days of our love in our marriage, or we might not have made it.

Most men would have tried to find comfort outside the home, but David stayed with me and our children constantly. It might have been because he was afraid of losing anyone else, but whatever the reason, it brought us closer than we've ever been, and I'm thankful for it.

Jennifer agrees with Elizabeth's perspective. *"It was very rough at first for Jim and me. We had to continue taking care of our other children in addition to seeing after the care of Nancy, and this took a lot out of both of us, but we worked together. We gave each other breaks when needed, and worked like a tag team.*

I know Jim was stressed out, having to go to work everyday, come home to help me with our children and our daily caretaking of Nancy, who is now an adult and still lives with us. He did all this with love and patience and never complained; who else but a chosen man of God would have taken on such chaos? Not many.

Although Kate has had some challenging relationships, she still believes there is definitely a chosen man out there for her, even though she hasn't quite met him yet.

"You have to kiss a few frogs to find your prince, but I've been lucky. The men who I've been involved with, have been able to look past the disability and appreciate my humor and intellect, and it's been more than just curiosity.

I don't know if there are men who are chosen, I just believe that there are men and women who can look beyond the outer shell to the inner "you" and those are few and far between. This is only true for some black men. My first husband, my son's father and I were together for 15 years until the relationship ended.

In many cases, it seems that most black men are only into having trophy wives or girlfriends. So it makes it that much more difficult for women with disabilities, because women like us aren't considered trophies, but as in every other area of my life, I don't give up easily.

My second husband was white and we met at an international rehabilitation conference in Switzerland, when I worked in the mayor's office, as a liaison.

My friend, Peter was there with me and brought over a delegate from Switzerland, named Barry who was white and a quadriplegic. Peter introduced Barry to me and we soon became fast friends. Shortly after, we were married and it was great--for a while. This lasted for about a year, because Barry decided he was too old for a relationship, so the marriage ended, and that's the way it goes.

Overall, I believe I've been blessed to have some meaningful relationships—even though they didn't last as long as I would have liked. Whether we're disabled or not, I do believe that God intends for everyone to experience love and puts us in a position to meet each other. I got a wonderful son out of the first marriage and a great time in Switzerland out of the second—so I'm not complaining and my "Mr. Right" is still out there!"

Being of the same spirit is how a woman can tell if she has found her chosen man Helga says, but she cautions you have to be careful and let God bring them to you and be sure it's God doing the matching.

"You have to find someone with whom you're compatible in every area—someone made specifically for you, with similar personalities, character, goals and spirit. You have to be able to speak the same language and communicate on every level—especially spiritually, there's no replacement for that, and even though it may take some time, believe me, it's definitely worth the wait.

I've learned through experience, that women looking for soul mates need to move slowly and in the direction in which we hear God speak as he leads us to our own special chosen man. This is critical. Knowing who we're getting involved with takes some time and some real interconnection. Just like He does in every other aspect of our lives, God does direct us to our chosen man, but in due time and in due season. However, in many cases, we tend to ignore Him because that man doesn't come in the package we want or have all or most of the characteristics (being fit, fine and full of fortune, etc.) we thought we wanted.

Today, finding love and true relationships is hard for everyone, but for women with special needs kids who are looking for love and stability, it's that much harder. Too many times, men can't see past our children and their needs and run away. Then sometimes, out of desperation and loneliness, we tend to look for love in all the wrong places. However, as women of strength and resolve in every other area, we've got to be the same when it comes to finding love...never give up and never give in.

I believe it is possible for all of us to find our chosen man, if we take the time to listen to that quiet voice inside and hear the call of God's wisdom. This can happen at any age, and in any circumstance. It will help us all avoid a lot of unnecessary pain, and I'm at a point in my life where I'm willing to wait."

"Only God knows His chosen man for His chosen woman...the key is having the self love, confidence, patience and faith to wait him out!

87

UNCONDITIONAL LOVE

No matter what the circumstances
Your love remains strong
Like you, they're not perfect
But you know some things are wrong
But your love shines through,
Holding them no matter what
Because in more cases than you'd like,
You are all that they've got
As your special child blossoms like a beautiful
*   spring flower*
You learn how to live and enjoy life,
Minute by minute, hour by hour
Unconditional love is what you feel and display
Truly meant from the heart and is God's special
*   way*
Of showing this love is not just for your child,
Who can laugh and enjoy life's simple things,
Yet has such a long way to go,
But also for those watching in awe,
Many of whom you don't even know
The wonder from where and
From whom you get the strength
To go the distance, to go the length
But to God be the glory, for they can't help but see
His love giving you hope for whatever life brings
And your love for those imperfect, will forever be

Chapter Six
Unconditional Love

"And now abide faith, hope, love these three, but the greatest of these is love." 1 Corinthians 13:13

In this day and age, where things seem to have gone haywire, where everything that was once right has become wrong and everything that was once wrong has become right, the one thing that remains constant is God's unconditional love for all his children—disabled or not.

I'm sure it pains him to witness so many of us putting limitations and conditions on those we love and not even knowing how to love. This was never His plan—especially when it comes to those who love and serve Him. We're supposed to serve as examples to those who don't know Him, and how much He loves us unconditionally, with every spot and with every wrinkle. That's how God intended His children to treat each other, with love unconditional.

Unconditional love does not just have to be between a biological mother and child, man and wife, or people who are related at all. It could be just for people…known or unknown—for a long time or for a short time, popular or not, with a lot of resources or with none.

Again, Ruth and Naomi from the bible are what I consider to be great examples of loving God and each other, unconditionally despite the hardships they both encountered. Neither one acted like victims of circumstance, nor did they blame or curse God for their misfortune. They just loved each other unconditionally and were there for each other when needed, no matter what.

Both were from different nations and of different faiths, yet they did not ostracize or try to hurt one another, but accepted each other for who they were, went through the difficult times together and blessed each other when their circumstances changed and/or improved. Although they're not women, I can't help but think of Jonathan and David from the bible. Jonathan was King Saul's son who was kind of disabled. He had a problem with one of his feet that made him limp, I think back in the day they called it a club foot, for which he was made to feel ashamed by those around him.

However, David loved him unconditionally and there was a true, loving friendship between the two, almost from the time they met and they were like brothers to each other. They protected each other through dangerous times, had fun with each other, were there for each other and remained this way until Jonathan's untimely death. This is the way it should be for everyone in God's family.

We're supposed to treat each member of each family from every race, culture, ethnic group, economic background, etc., lovingly and unconditionally no matter what their problem or situation. Unfortunately, this doesn't always happen. Surprisingly, even within the same family, children with special needs are not as embraced as other children.

David and Jonathan were not even related and had an unconditional love for one another. Jonathan, who was the king's son, didn't even have this kind of love with his own father and vice versa. It hurts me to say, but today there are some very sad and painful stories heard in the news of the lack of love and caring to people in general, young and old. But it seems sometimes for the physically and mentally challenged child or adult, more unnecessary violence is unleashed towards them without reason.

The true compassion, protection and support that should be offered by "the system," doesn't really exist—at least not in the manner it should. We hear many cases all over the country, of children abused in a variety of ways...sometimes even by their own family members. Incidentally, these children by are not always mentally or physically challenged.

Just like God chose these special mothers (and their mates) I also believe in many cases, He selects those who closely surround them and interacts with them regularly with a special kindness, strength and dependability. This allows parents of these children to do what they are called to do, and that is to help these children live as normal and as productive a life as possible.

Grandparents, for example, are among these warm, dependable and unconditionally loving people. As they would with any grandchild, most grandparents immediately fall in love their special needs children wholeheartedly and many times all the more-- with each blemish, spot or wrinkle or imperfection they may possess.

Loving Sierra unconditionally is not only true for Sierra's dad and me, but is also true of her grandparents, her older brother Steven (my stepson) and all her aunts, uncles and cousins. They loved her as soon as she came into the world and even more so when they realized she had special needs. As they do with anyone else, they accept her for who she is.

Sierra's paternal grandparents, for example, love Sierra unconditionally and are somewhat overly protective of her—just like they are with all their grandchildren. They tend to spoil her and she loves all the attention. Her grandfather is "Pop Pop" and both her grandmothers are "Ma Ma," whom she named herself. Grandma Stanley, my husband's mother, is especially attentive.

"I am in constant prayer for Sierra and I pray that anyone—adult or otherwise, who comes in contact with her or other children with similar mental or physical challenges, is kind, patient and

understanding.

We love all our grandchildren dearly, but Sierra holds a special place in our hearts. She's always so happy, excited about life, and loving and we can feel that love emanating from her whenever we see her or talk to her on the phone.

I hate the idea of people taking advantage of these children. It's one of the things that bother me the most about how the disability community is treated. It's scary to say, but unfortunately there are some terrible people living in our society. I must admit, I really have to pray about having unconditional love for people who would mistreat innocent children, it's not easy, but I'm working on it.

Sharing Deserving Discipline with Deserving Love

Providing respite services at home allowed Helga to lovingly dispense discipline to those in her care, resulting in their growth and development, but she wasn't so adamant about discipline, when it came to her son; but says she continues to work hard to change her behavior in that area.

"Loving your child unconditionally does not mean spoiling them, and I know what it's like to want to love your disabled child to the point where you begin to pamper them too much. This is in no way

good for them—you know what they say about having too much of a good thing!

Too much love can also have a negative affect. I realized this as soon as my son went to live with another family when he became an adult. This was one of the hardest decisions I ever made—although it will only be temporary. Since going to live with the other family, however, he really started to become more independent.

He lost weight, he was walking more, he was doing things he hadn't done at home, because I pampered him too much. So that I don't stunt his rapidly increasing development, I am working on the temptation to pamper him whenever he's around me, so I don't undo the good that is being done through his new caregivers.

In fact, Helga says that her daughters have also displayed their unconditional love for their brother from day one, by taking care of him, as well as their mother does.

"I know many families who shy away and even run from dealing with a family member who is disabled, but I'm pleased to say that my daughters are not like that. They both have made me very proud by sharing their own unique ways of displaying their deep love and affection for their brother, Moses. His disability doesn't hinder them from treating him like any older and younger sister would—except they have to take more care of him

than most sisters.

I know it hasn't been easy for them because there aren't too many things that he can do on his own, but they never complain. If they're caring for him while I'm away, they will bathe him, take him to the bathroom and prepare meals for him, as he can feed himself. He was a hefty child and has grown into a strapping young man, so it's not easy, but they do what they can to help their brother who knows that he is definitely loved no matter what.

This was not just with their brother. There have been many times when they have shown their compassion towards other children with mild to severe physical and mental disabilities, whose parents I'd provide care giving and respite services. They would sometimes take time to help me care for these children, just as well as they helped care for their brother.

I really applaud them for this, because today, it's very rare to find unconditional love in young people like that and I can't help but be proud of the fact that I must have done something right in raising them."

The love of Kate's family and the love of her teachers when she was younger, are among Kate's fondest and truest examples of offering and sharing unconditional love with her.

"My son has always been remarkable almost from the day he was born. As soon as he could, he always worked to be independent, supportive and

patient—never making me to feel as if there was anything at all different from any of his other friends' mothers.

I also have been blessed to have a family as "crazy" as I am, and I use that term affectionately. I have always handled my struggles with humor, which is part of my personality and I'm glad that is also the case with most of my family.

My mother encouraged me to use my intelligence and my wit. I've heard her say that I came out the womb talking and she always pushed me to have opinions and to share them. I love and thank her very much for treating me as she did any of her other children, and I appreciate her continued support of me no matter what. That to me is unconditional love.

I also remember another example of unconditional love and caring that was displayed by one of my teachers—not just for me, but for all the other students in her small special education class. Actually, she is someone with whom I still keep in touch to this day.

I was the first black person in a special education class in Atlanta and it was a time when special education was really special...they really educated us. My teacher was selected to take a special education class in upstate New York at Syracuse University, so she could work with us more intently. She did an awesome job with us and I'm thankful that she had high expectations of all us and challenged us.

We were taught reading, writing and arithmetic just like everyone else. We were also taught poetry, art, music and everything all the other students at school were learning, preparing to live as productive adults. I learned how to type at age seven-years-old and we were taken on field trips like to the symphony, museums and other cultural places.

The unconditional love displayed by people like my family and this teacher, made me believe that all things were possible. These are people who never gave up on me and who pushed me be more than what others thought I would be. It was because of them not treating me any different than anyone else that has made me who I am today.

And who I am today is a very determined and strong willed person fighting for the quiet voices of those with disabilities, both children and adults, so they could have the same opportunities I had and more. I can't tell you how much I love and appreciate those who had a significant impact on my life, who encouraged me and believed in me. I want to be able to help share that spirit with others, so they can pass it on."

"The key to unconditional love is to share the true love of God that you have with anyone, at any time, for any reason, no matter what...and experiencing the joy and gift of life while sharing it."

DYING TO SELF,
TO FIND MYSELF

My thoughts were once was all about me
Considering myself all that and a bag of chips
Strutting my stride, swinging my hips,
I turned the heads of many a guy
And never even questioned why, because I knew
I was me, on my way to all I could be
Certain I had it all, never even hearing the call
To serve one brought from my womb
Who could not speak, walk or use a spoon
Angry at first, nothing could quench the thirst
Of dreams and visions yet to be fulfilled
I know the old me has died with a new
Me taking her place, instead of running
God has taken me out of the race
To exceed and excel like all the others
'Cause I'm not like the other mothers
It wasn't until I let myself die
That I finally found myself and understood why
My call is my purpose, now being regaled
To remind others that their ship hasn't sailed
But in dying to ourselves, we find who we are
We're not below, but as high and bright as heaven's
    stars
And our dreams don't have to disappear
Just look up and inside, and behold...we are there!

Chapter Seven
Dying To Self To Find Myself

...For to me, to live is Christ, and to die is gain...Philipians 1:21

There was a time when I thought I had the world at my feet. Everything I'd prayed for from a little girl, teenager and young woman was coming to pass. I held executive positions, ate at fine restaurants, wore designer clothes and shoes, God reunited me with an old boyfriend, who is now my husband. Life was going great and would stay that way—or so I thought.

I soon had to discover a whole new me, one I didn't even know existed. I had never been a selfish person (at least I didn't think so), but always wanted my life to be a certain way-- and it was just the way I had planned, for a certain amount of time, but like the bible says… "time and chance happen to them all."

Having come a long way from being an extremely shy, yet extremely determined person, I liked myself, where I was going and I looked forward to the future. Just like Debbie, I wasn't used to things not going according to plan. I soon found out that no matter how well you think you have things in place, one never really knows the plans God has for you. So we might as well just sit back, take a deep breath and do what we can to enjoy what we could, while we could and not try to resist the journey—it makes it that much harder. But in the end, it's all worth it.

I guess that's the way Moses' mother (the one from the bible) Jochebed may have felt. I'm sure it wasn't in her plan to have to send her son away to keep him from being killed, to give him up to another woman to raise and serve as his wet nurse just to be close to him. I'm sure this must have caused her tremendous pain, nonetheless, as a result of her selflessness, whether she realized it or not, her actions would be marked in history and change the life of millions of people, freeing them from bondage, through her son.

By dying to herself, by letting what she felt was best for her be put on the back burner, to do what was best for her son and others, Jochebed unknowingly changed the course of history, and by doing so, opened the door for others to do the same throughout the centuries.

As mothers of special needs children, at first we are filled with shock and pain when we first find out about our child's mental and or physical challenges. That in itself is a rude awakening to many of us. But in order for both mother and their special children to do more than subsist, we as mothers had to get past what we wanted as individuals, not only for the sake of our children, but for our own sakes. How you manage your crisis may help someone else manage theirs. We had to die to ourselves to find ourselves.

We never know who's watching, noticing how strong or how weak we are in overwhelming situations, and how we're influencing them. As for me, I didn't know that I was having a tremendous spiritual influence on my family. I didn't know how closely they were watching to see how I handled it all, where I got the strength. When I shared that it was God that gave me strength, they soon began to look to me for spiritual guidance and prayer. This was yet another assignment God had for me.

After having Sierra and learning of her challenges, it was then that I began to see the dreams of my youth fading fast and I must say I wasn't too happy about it. I loved my daughter and she came first in my life, so for a little while, all the things I wanted and had worked years to achieve, had to be put aside.

As a result of my decision, and as the years went by, I found that I had more in me than just being the hired help for someone else's company. I had talent, I had drive and I had a burning desire and motivation, to make sure Sierra had the best life possible. So I put what I'd learned professionally all those years to work for me and began consulting from my home office. Stepping out on my own had never crossed my mind before, but having left my job to care for Sierra, I needed to do something to help out financially at home.

It turned out to be the best decision I could have made. I am happier, healthier and have returned to following my dreams, but on God's time schedule first, and mine second, according to His plan, not anyone else's.

By turning away from what I thought I wanted, Sierra is better for it, I am better for it and I believe the many people with which God has allowed me to come in contact and influence, are better for it. It all has helped to like the "self" I had become, by dying to my old self.

New Challenges Result in New Choices

As mothers of special needs children, we all can attest to the fact that we tend to wonder when and how everything in our lives had gone haywire. Over a period of time, we accepted the fact that because of our new circumstances, things would be a little difficult for us for awhile. But we didn't realize how much of ourselves we would have to give up. However, because we loved our children and wanted what was best for them, we soon discovered we really had no choice. Something was going to have to go.

Just as I did, Helga, Debbie, and Elizabeth have experienced their own challenges in dying to their former selves to find out who they really were inside. It may have taken immeasurable months, even years, but eventually, they did find out what they were capable of doing, and even had the talent to do, which in some cases, their old selves never would have even considered. Helga shared her transition with me.

"One of the main struggles that I had at the beginning of my son's life was trying not to focus too much on myself. It was a very difficult thing to do. I had to learn to put behind me the one thing I had hoped to be —a singer and entertainer. But as much as I wanted that, I wanted my son's healing more.

Sacrifice is what parenting is all about. We all still have dreams, goals and objectives we would like to see happen in our lives, and it's not to say that they won't, but sometimes God wants us to complete a task and then move on from there. That's when He opens the door for us to complete ourselves. In the meantime, we have to learn how to put our needs, and many of our wants, in a box until it's time to take them out again.

After a while that way of life becomes a normal part of who you are, especially when you're trying to live for God. I know that was the case with me and Moses. After I got over the shock of what I was going to have to deal with being a mother to Moses, I just did what I had to do...and was happy to do it, because he was my son.

The more I lived to see that my son had all he

needed, I started to think about the other parents going through the same thing, and how limited certain services were for families like mine. Again, I took the focus off my own family to see what I could do for others and it made a tremendous difference in my life.

Giving to others first, before I think about myself and what I need, is a natural part of who I am now. That's not to say that I completely ignore myself and what's necessary for me to have joy in my life, because I do have joy and contentment. What I don't do is ignore the needs of others, so I can have what I want, whether it's a family member or not.

I put my earlier pain, suffering and anger aside to help other mothers in my situation to find peace and hope, and I can't tell you how much it has changed me. Having been such a rebellious person, I had to squash the side of me that would rise up in anger and instead, lovingly reach out to even those who had hurt me in the past.

Was it easy? It most definitely wasn't, but in the end it was very rewarding. I saw doors open for me that I never would have believed I would experience in this lifetime. The whole thing taught me a great lesson. Lay yourself aside…if only for awhile. Now I'm moving in the direction in which I'd always wanted to go. I've returned to the music industry, my son is developing by leaps and bounds and so am I. I've re-discovered that I am smart and determined and I'm ready to take on the world—in a good way.

It may take a little time, but if we allow our fleshly selves to disappear and let our spirits be led by God, He gives us the patience and love to see it all through. He offers you new opportunities to spread your wings and fly. I've got to say that making a decision like this is no bowl of cherries, but if you give it a chance, life does get sweeter every day."

It's one thing to sacrifice your wants, needs and feelings for your own child or family members, but what if you had to do it for someone else, while still deeply traumatized by your own situation? That's what Elizabeth chose to do.

"An acquaintance of mine had a son who attended the same school our daughter Jada had attended. In fact, our children even dated for a very short while. Over a period of time, she realized that her son seemed to be having constant memory losses and when they went to check it out, the doctor said her son also had a brain tumor and needed surgery.

She called me frantic, crying and wanted to know how I was able to handle the heart rending situation with my own daughter. Although I was still in pain and suffering everyday because my daughter had been in a coma over a year now, I could relate to what she was feeling and didn't want her to suffer the way I did.

God gave me the strength as well as the desire to put myself and my worries aside and do what I could, to guide her through the day to day process of standing strong in her hour of crisis.

I shared with her little insights and methods on how to make things less stressful for her family. These were just small things, but they helped me get through it all tremendously, when I first found out about Jada. One way was to leave update messages on her answering machine for those who were concerned, so she wouldn't have to repeat the same things to people over and over again. Situations like ours are very trying to speak of, much less to repeat over and over.

It was a blessing to be able to be there for her, hold her hand, let her cry on my shoulder and know that I was helping someone, even if I couldn't help myself or my daughter at that time. It allowed me to think of something else and someone else besides the pain I was dealing with personally, and that helped me to get through in ways I couldn't have imagined. Somehow it eased the pain, if only a little bit.

The biggest and most important insight I could share with my friend, was that she had no choice but to lean on God. No one else could understand what she was going through the way He could—not even me. I also told her not to bother trying to get answers to the "why?" question, because that wouldn't help, because she may never get an answer.

After a few months, her son did recover and I was very happy for her child's recovery. She even came to me one day after it was over and thanked me saying that she felt more peace, comfort and strength being able to talk to me and share her pain and fear, as she went through her ordeal, because she knew I would understand as a mother going through the same thing.

It really made me happy to hear her say that. It helped me to know that I made a real difference in someone else's life during my own time of crisis. I know that was nothing but the grace of God to give me the strength to do that.

I could have been selfish, not listen to God speaking to me and not done anything to help her, because I had so much I was dealing with myself, but that's just not the kind of person I am. We are all on this road together and we have to make ourselves accessible. That sometimes means ignoring our own pain and sorrows and helping those who may need us -- in any way we can. We need to put ourselves aside, even be willing to carry and bear some traumatic situation for others, and that's exactly the way God wants us to treat one another. Why shouldn't we? He did so much more than that for us.

I don't exactly know what my future holds, but I can take comfort in knowing that I have a strength, a love and a power inside me, that can help change lives for the better, a power only derived from the holy spirit. And that's an awesome, encouraging, *comforting and lifting spirit to have. It's helped me through many a day and many a night.*

"A new you is born when your old self dies, allowing the phoenix inside you, to rise..."

NEVER GIVE UP!
MIRACLES DO HAPPEN

Staring out the window at night in despair
The reality of life too painful to bear
No more laughter in your voice
No more sparkle in your eyes
In the dark of night, only God hears your cries
Yet somehow in the distance, you see the light
You know deep down, it's going to be alright
As you keeping moving toward,
Keep pushing straight ahead,
You hear the silent voice of God speak
And your heart being quietly led
To know that you know your prayers have been
    answered
And that all good things come to those who wait
Yes, even on this earthly side of Heaven's gate
It has taken a while, and yes it did tarry
But all your burdens He was able to carry
Yes, miracles do happen, as did yours, so rejoice!
Praise our God with a resounding voice
Praise the Lord everybody! Raise your queen's
    golden cup
Celebrate the fact that though tears, pain and hurt,
As much as you wanted to, you never, ever gave up!

Chapter Eight
Never Give Up! Miracles Do Happen

And let us not grow weary while doing good, for in due season we shall reap, if we do not lose heart...Galations 6:9

The bible has many stories of elected ladies who never gave up, who never lost heart, even though their circumstances looked dim, not knowing for sure if they would receive the miracles for which they were waiting from God. Imagine if Sarah, Abraham's wife had given up, believing that at 90 years old, she would not be able to have a child, but she did—despite her age.

And then there was Hannah who was distraught because she too thought she was infertile, but after many years and many prayers, she was blessed by God with a baby—which she dedicated back to God.

These are just two examples of women who with all evidence to the contrary, did not give up and eventually got the miracle for which they were praying, even though it took more than a little time.

It is said that God's time is not our time, but we can't escape the fact that we still wish He would just hurry up and make it happen already! Life can be extremely painful, and there are many moments when we just can't take the constant struggles anymore and say to ourselves (and sometimes to others), "This is just too hard, I give up!"

But I've come to understand that we can't rush God and that nothing happens until He says it is to happen. Not until it's our season. In fact, in most cases, giving up is the worse thing we could do—no matter how impossible things may seem, because just when we decide to give up, and actually do give up, that's exactly when the blessing we've been waiting for appears.

I know I've been there a time or two, myself and came very close to throwing it all away...my marriage, my family, my career and my hopes and dreams and just walk away from it all. But something inside just wouldn't let me do it. I've never been a quitter, so I couldn't do it even if I wanted to. This is a characteristic and a blessing that my mother passed down to all her children, so I kept going and I've been blessed because of it. It all began by watching my mother and by hearing God speak to me through her.

A woman who had been through some very trying and heartbreaking times, Mom never stopped fighting for her children. What I saw by watching her was that her faith in God and her passion to make some positive changes for her children and even for herself, would not let her quit.

In a way she reminded me of some of the many memorable women in the bible. She was strong willed and relentless, like Sarah; she was determined to escape poverty like Naomi and Ruth; she was intelligent and independent like Rahab, Miriam and Tamar. She was also very feisty and not one to mess with and I'm happy to say all of her five daughters, including me, are a lot like her.

Women like us—strong, relentless, determined women, don't give up very easily. We go after what we want and generally, we get it. I can't say that we don't encounter some disappointments or loss in our lives, because we do. However when we do, most of us just shake the dust off after falling, get up and start all over again.

This is true particularly of elected ladies on assignment by God—whether we're mothers of special needs children or not. We may not realize it at first, but we soon find out how important we are in the scheme of things. We affect families, our friends, our workplace, our communities, and generally touch everyone with whom we come in contact, in one way or another.

Not that we especially like it, but there always seems to be quite a few people depending on us. Whether we realize it or not, we are leaders who are not easily discouraged or dissuaded, offering positive and powerful examples to those quietly observing.

Wishing for miracles are not how miracles come to pass…although God does allow them to occur when we least expect them now and then—and they're always right on time. But for the most part for miracles happen, besides lots of prayer, we need to take steps and make decisions to bring them to fruition. It takes hard work and continuous effort and there's no getting around it.

I've heard pastors say over and over, that God has already done his part and the rest is up to us. Well finding our miracles takes some grit and gumption, persistence and pressing until we reach our goals—whatever they may be. It's almost like giving birth-- we have to labor for our baby's entrance into the world and keep pushing and pushing until it appears. But in order for us to see the miracles we're hoping for, we can't afford to ever give up.

Continuous disappointment, rejection, betrayal, self pity, trials, pitfalls, tribulations and negativity can sap the strength of anyone and cause us all to lose faith. However, with God's grace, He gives us the strength to keep going, not stopping and giving it everything we've got. With His guidance we can do all things, but it all begins with our faith—faith in ourselves, faith in God and in the power He's given us.

It may be a stretch, but we have to learn how to lean on our faith to be able to spot our miracles when they come along, because some miracles are not visible. Some miracles are every day events that others take for granted, but these are miraculous events for the millions of women with special needs children.

Giving Up Means Missing Out

Something as simple as seeing your child begin to walk without assistance at 10 years old or older, is a miracle. It's also a miracle hearing them say their first intelligible word past the age of six, when at that age other children are talking and reading. Those are simple things in the order of most parents' lives, yet they are miracles for those who recognize them and don't see them as soon as we'd like, but we're just happy to see them.

I'll never forget when our daughter, Sierra first said "Mommy" and "Daddy." She was around five years old, and to us, those were two of the most beautiful words we had ever heard. It didn't happen at the same time, but when they did, those were glorious times for us and we rejoiced and were glad in it. Today at 18, she may not be able to say many words, but she has tremendous comprehension, can follow many instructions, and follows her own initiative such as bringing me the phone when she hears it ring—(or sometimes even before it rings).

She gets up, goes to where the phone is and brings it back to me. She also likes to bring the phone to me because she sees that I'm on it all the time when I'm working. The fact that she's thinking and acting on those thoughts, are miracles to me and I thank God for them. I look back at her photos when she was a toddler taking early infant stimulation therapy, and I see the determination on her face to accomplish what the teachers were instructing her to do.

She is even more determined now to walk, talk, write, read and do everything she sees other children and adults doing. Just as any other teenager, when she feels like being alone and wants her privacy, she shuts the door to her bedroom behind us after we've come into her room to help her with something. I love when she does that! It may be minor to you, but it's major to me.

There are so many other goals and accomplishments Sierra has attained as she continues to grow and develop physically and mentally. These are events and instances we consider miraculous and are very thankful that they are becoming more and more frequent as she gets older. She's going to be an awesome testimony to the work of God some day and her father and I are looking forward to that day.

The same goes for Helga and Debbie and I'm sure a host of other mothers with children like ours, who have experienced miracles in one way or another. As a result, we are all the more excited and more expectant of something new occurring with our children every day. Helga recalls distinctly when as a baby, doctors counted Moses off and wanted her to do the same.

"I smile whenever I think back to when Moses was a baby and the doctors told me all the things he wouldn't be able to do--that he would be a vegetable. Contrary to what they said, I chose to believe the report of the Lord, who told me he would have some comprehension, he would walk, no longer have seizures and do so much more as time passed.

Just as God said, today Moses has wonderful comprehension, is saying a few words, prays before each meal, walks and feeds himself. He may not have started doing these things later in life, but he's doing them now and that's all that counts. Every day is a miracle and every accomplishment Moses makes, no matter how small, is a miracle for me."

Debbie could relate to Helga's joy in seeing her son achieve what are minor milestones for some, but were major ones for her and her family.

"Terrance has accomplished so much more than the doctors thought he would and is as proud of himself as we are of him, about accomplishing the things he's worked so hard to do. Like we have always wanted and believed, he's showing everyone he encounters that he won't allow his life to be short changed in any way, just because he was born with a physical disability.

He is doing so many amazing things that even his extended family wasn't sure he'd be able to do, such as get a job. But he does have one and takes the para-transit bus to and from work a few times a week.

Terrance may not be where other young men are in their early 20's, and may not be able to do many of the things they do, but he is developing into a very capable young man every day, working hard to have a great future. He loves who he is and loves life. We consider those things miracles and are looking forward to much more."

"The wonder of seeing constant miracles comes from never giving up or giving in, until each one appears."

ARISE, SHINE YOUR LIGHT HAS COME!

Arise Shine! For your light has come!
The glory of the Lord is risen upon you
Take no thought to fear of those whispering in your
ear
Saying you don't have what it takes
You might as well just give it up
Trying to discourage you, but only for their sakes
They're just afraid of the success you've made
Because how dare you strive to rise above it all
Seeking independence by following your call
Wanting to make a great impact, since a small girl
Not knowing God formed you, to go into the world
And with His guidance, help others break free
To find the treasure hidden within you all,
Your light is shining for all to see
Giving praise unto God as He holds your hand
Having done all you know to do, just stand
Your time is now, walk through opportunities' gate
Arise, shine for our light has come
Your purpose within your dreams await
Slowly, but unforgettably rising, like the dawning of
the sun
It's your fate and life's battle you have won!

Chapter Nine

Arise, Shine,
For Your Light has Come

Arise, shine; for your light has come! And the glory of the Lord is risen upon you...Isaiah 60:1

One of my favorite scriptures in the bible is Isaiah 60:1—"Arise, shine for your light has come! And the glory of the Lord is risen upon you...." I think I came across that scripture when I was having a particularly difficult time, feeling sorry for myself professionally and personally and I was searching for something to ease my discouragement, because to tell you the truth, I was about to lose it.

It was very strange really, because the first time I saw it, I just happened to open the bible and there the scripture was, right in front of me, speaking to me loud and clear and I knew that was God trying to talk to me. The chapter shared many encouraging words about my future, about where I was going, what I was doing and that my hard work in all areas of my life, was about to bring me a harvest.

There was something about those first few words that captured my heart and my soul—Arise, shine; for our light has come! They gave me hope, excited me and spoke to me personally.

During that time, my mother lost her mother, our grandmother, who was 92-year-old. Not only that, but my daughter began having seizures we hadn't seen for years. Since we hadn't seen one in so long, we had hoped they had gone away forever, but it seemed like they were coming back. Then I found out that out my very successful older brother whom I'd always looked up to as a model of success, was going through his own traumas—physical, mental, emotional and financial.

He had became extremely depressed after having lost his prestigious job in the movie industry. Not only was he going through a divorce, but his health began to decline—mostly from mental stress. In addition, his consulting business never really took off the way he'd expected.

That's not all, a year or so later, his ex-wife died unexpectedly and she was someone whom he really loved -- as we all did. However for some reason we didn't understand, she chose not to keep in touch with us after the divorce, and we never heard from her again until we learned of her passing. It wasn't long after that it seemed he just gave up fighting and went to be with the Lord only six months after Julia did, at only 55.

I remember him saying sadly one day not long before he died, *"I've wasted so much time, so much money and so much love. If only had I known where I'd end up, I would have done things differently."* Hearing him say those things was all too overwhelming for me and I never thought that he only had a few short months after that conversation.

As a result, I became depressed, but no one knew it because I hid it well. At the time, my life wasn't going as well as I had hoped it would be by my late thirties, but what my brother experienced was a wake up call from God—one that I needed to see, hear and experience, so I wouldn't make the same mistakes.

But I didn't know how to come out of it. I didn't really like myself around that time. My drive and ambition had disappeared and procrastination had become my comfort. Somehow it became easier to put things off, than dealing with them immediately. I knew I had to do something about the state I was in, or I would be stuck in a pit for the rest of my life.

I had lost my usual positive mindset and was in bondage to myself. I knew that if I didn't break free and go after my goals and the things I've dreamed about, one day it would be too late and I would have missed my opportunity.

The thought of my being one of those people who died without realizing their dreams, with their treasures still buried within them, just terrified me. Knowing there were people who missed out on their destinies because they didn't go after them deeply saddened me, because I felt I was close to doing the same thing.

And when I read that scripture "Arise Shine, For Your Light Has Come," it was like a light bulb had been turned on in my head, and a voice calling out from within telling me that it wasn't too late and I could change the direction my life had taken.

What We Want Tends To Hide In Who We Are

So I took a good, hard look at myself and saw all the areas in which I needed to improve. I did an about face and it sure wasn't easy. I began exercising self control in every area. I ate less and exercised more, I thought things through and made better decisions, rather than doing things hastily. And, I guess most importantly, I began holding myself accountable for the situation I was in, which came from not moving when I should have and missing out on opportunities unnecessarily.

I didn't know it then, but my actions all stemmed from my fear of success. There were some directions in which I knew in my heart that I should have been taking, but was too afraid to take them, because (and I know this is strange), but I didn't take them because I knew I would be successful at them. I now know that this is a common trap that many people fall in, but didn't realize I was one of those people.

It has been said that when God gives you a vision, he gives you the provision, and the minute I renewed my mind and made up in my mind that I would go after the things I loved most, my life started to change. I began to diligently pursue my passion for ingesting books on self improvement. I also began pursuing my passion for writing and my passion for music. These all led to doors opening for me to realize my dreams of becoming an author, songwriter and singer—all of which I am now enjoying.

By developing more self confidence and stepping out on faith, my friends who knew of my love for singing, helped to find opportunities for me to sing. In addition, because of my new frame of mind and new attitude, I found myself slowly but surely, being referred more and securing larger PR assignments. Things were really starting to look up.

What I discovered, is that the ability to open these doors was always there, already within me, but I didn't move on them. I stayed in my numb state hesitating to take some action, using life, work, money and Sierra as excuses. It was now time to put up or shut up. So I did just that and found out that I had been hiding behind a façade of being a strong, 'take no crap' woman. In some degree and in certain areas, that was the truth, especially when it came to my daughter, but not really when it came to me.

It was during this time that I met my best friend,

Helga, who I believe was another part of God's grand design for propelling me into my future and in helping me to "arise, shine."

It is because that divine connection, that I believe God's call for me became clear. I was supposed to use my marketing background to assist her in reaching her goals with her non-profit organization. Her purpose was to develop an organization to help other women like ourselves receive the specific and unavailable assistance they needed to care for their children. This was something for which I had a real passion and with which I could relate, so I went for it and it's been one blessing after another ever since.

As an added bonus, it turned out Helga was also a talented professional singer and songwriter with years of experience. So we shared and exchanged areas of expertise and combined them when necessary, and began to see our individual and collective endeavors take off. Before long, we both could hear God talking to us to let no more time pass, but to arise and shine because our light had definitely come. Here is some of her experience:

"I've had a relationship with God from a very early age because I had to, God was the only one I could count on...if it wasn't for Him, I wouldn't have gotten through it and I probably wouldn't be here today. I absolutely believe that God was directing my life and has been doing so since my childhood, because there was a time that due to my

anger, I put myself in some very precarious situations. I got involved with some unsavory and potentially dangerous people, but God protected me.

Then I got married and had three beautiful children—including my son, Moses. In fact, Moses is the main reason that I have kept on pushing the way that I have. My daughters can take care of themselves, but I want to make sure that my son is taken care properly and that he is safe, secure and happy—whether I'm here or not.

So I'm fighting with the gifts and talents God has given me, to make sure that happens. After a long and difficult struggle, it's all starting to come together.

Despite the nay sayers, my visions and dreams are coming to pass. Who would have thought that I'd be the founder and CEO of a growing non-profit organization, certainly not me! But I believe All Children Are Special, Inc., will make a difference in the lives of families with special needs children all over the country—as it has already begun to do in mine.

With my dream of becoming a singer and recording artist materializing, I am proud to be singing the kinds of songs I love, songs which I hope will inspire and motivate listeners who don't know God, to want to find out more about Him, and for those who do know Him, how to hold on to their faith and never let go. But at the same time, my dream and my ministry is helping other women to realize they no longer have to be held captive to the misery, pain and uncertainty in their lives, because there are incredibly wonderful times head, but only God can light the way.

Now I know why that line of scripture Isaiah 60, "Arise shine for your light has come, and the glory of the Lord is risen upon you," meant so much to me. It was letting me know that in order to achieve the lives for which we are all searching, we all have to get up, get out and get going so that the dreams we have always wanted will happen. But we have to make it happen, with God's help.

As we move forward in life, God's love inwardly tells when it's our turn to exceed and excel in the areas in which he gave us talent, and for which He had prepared us from the very beginning. Even though we're mothers, whether we have special needs children or not, and no matter what age, God wants us to know how important our days are, and that we shouldn't lose them to sorrow. And once we realize it for ourselves, it's our responsibility to help others do the same thing.

"Time not maximized, fear not destroyed and dreams not sought, keeps us from rising to occasions to let our outward strength grow and our inner light shine."

VICTORY IN THE CHALLENGE- -JOY COMES IN THE MORNING!

It may not seem like it right now, but tomorrow is a
new day
Your life may seem turned upside down
Not knowing what you did,
But feel you've been made to pay
Take heart in this truth, even if life gets in your way
That weeping may endure for a night
But joy comes in the morning!
Whatever it is, it too shall pass, although it seems
forever
Your angels surround you, keeping you safe
Their wings are your cover
Fighting through the muck and mire
To secure help for your child, your own
Don't worry, you have victory,
God knows the seeds that you've sown
Take heart in this truth, while you continue to fight
Joy comes in the morning, after weeping endures in
the night
A new day is here, put aside the fear
That you can't take the pressure or the strife
You're stronger than you think and your angels stay
near
Remember this, when life seems too hard to bear
Just as the sun sets and returns colorfully dawning
So will you soon be able to share
That weeping may endure for a night,
But joy does come in the morning!

Chapter Ten
Victory in the Challenge/
Joy Comes in the Morning!

But thanks be to God, who gives us the victory through our Lord Jesus Christ. Therefore, my beloved brethren, be steadfast, immovable, always abounding in the work of the Lord, knowing that your labor is not in vain in the Lord...1 Corinthians 15:57-58

Weeping may endure for a night, but joy comes in the morning...Psalm 30:5

Why is it that people, especially women—do not seem to realize just how strong they really are until their backs are against the wall? The fact is that we can handle almost any challenge but it's not until we're faced with it, that we realize we can handle it!

I know that in my case and most probably in the lives of women everywhere, if we're backed up into a corner, we find some way to fight our way out; in doing so, we become much more assertive, more confident and more successful women.

Despite our various challenges, by staying

faithful to God through our adversity, we are eventually rewarded for our faithfulness because He had been watching the whole time.

The fact of the matter is, we are all awesome, powerful women and with God's help, have learned to turn our misery into our ministries. This is what happens to elected ladies all over the world--those known and those yet unknown. Nationally renowned and elected ladies like media mogul Oprah Winfrey, pastor Paula White, singer Tina Turner and many others, can attest to experiencing some traumatic episodes in their lives. However, they used those experiences to fuel their current successes and assist other women in finding theirs.

As elected ladies of special needs children, we all need to follow their example and do the same. As a result of those ladies allowing themselves to get past their own painful history, they are helping millions of other women all around the world do the same thing—and so can we.

As mothers of special needs children, we are dealing with some of the most heart rending obstacles that exists for a mother, but our determination and fight inspires others to fight also—no matter what their struggle. Our job is to recognize that our purpose here is not to look back and ask questions about "why?" but look to our future and the future of our children, and see areas we can offer assistance and ask "why not?"

We should be serving as real examples to each other and women everywhere of what Apostle Paul was saying in Philippians 3:13. "Brethren, I do not count myself to have been apprehended; but one thing I do, forgetting those things which are behind and reaching forward to those things which are ahead."

God chose us because of a strength he knew was within us—that He himself put there. A strength that could be drawn upon when necessary, enabling us to put aside the hurt, pain, rejection and trauma associated with mothering and caring for children like ours. This is a struggle that not too many women have enough heart, fortitude, stamina or survival instincts to handle.

My own sister, who is a Lieutenant Colonel in the army and also a nurse, is a very strong woman. She has seen some extremely painful and devastating things happen to people in the hospital day in and day out, and her job is to care for these people and nurse them back to recovery. One week I went to visit her with Sierra and although she had seen me with Sierra before, this time she had to watch Sierra for a short time while I went out, and I believe it was quite an eye-opener for her.

When I returned she watched me change my young adult daughter's clothes, take her to the bathroom, give her a bath and do just about everything for her, including deciphering what she was saying. All she could say was "I don't know how you do it, but I know I couldn't."

Having seen that look before on countless people when we take Sierra to the mall, to the movies or to restaurants in her wheelchair, I just smiled and laughingly said to lighten the sadness in her voice, "It's alright, I'm used to it...you'd be surprised of what you're able to do when you love someone enough. And as you know, no one can love a child and do things for a child, like their mother."

Although others don't see it, we know that our victories may not come overnight, but they do come. Among the moments I consider as victories was when she learned how to make a peanut butter and jelly sandwich all by herself ; or when she went to the prom (her first date) with Helga's son, Moses—both in their wheelchairs and both all dressed up in their formal finery. That was another victory, for both moms. Moses even brought Sierra a rose at the door--you know that one made us both cry.

Watching her grow and develop into a young woman with determination to learn, love and live life to the best of her current ability are victories that fill me with joy. Some might consider these very simple things, but they mean the world to mothers like us.

When it comes to me personally, all I can say is I'm very excited about the direction in which my life is headed. As I mentioned earlier, I've been blessed for the better part of my life. But I'm really just finding out what I am supposed to be doing, what my purpose is and how to use my gifts and talents to propel me into my destiny. I see it happening very clearly; my having Sierra is what is bringing this all to pass (my books, my music, my business), and there's no words to express the joy and excitement I am feeling these days.

Although it's not completely over, this whole experience has taught me how to successfully maneuver through the dark pathways of my life and not lose myself in the process. I've also learned that I didn't have to understand everything to find my way.

In addition, I've learned how to celebrate small victories and be thankful for them and that sometimes God will deliver us from challenges immediately, and sometimes he will take us through them. As for me, the last 18 years have not been easy, but I'm glad to say that I'm more than on my way to the other side of through.

Helga, Elizabeth, Kate, Debbie and Jennifer can also attest to going through the fire and coming out on the other side, singed but not burned.

Helga explains her journey forward, full of excitement and expectancy for the coming years.

"As I move forward in life, I must say that I am rather proud of myself because I see how far I've come from where I had been and I know how close I am to the place I've always wanted to go. I'm very proud of what I've been able to accomplish thus far.

I'm using my passion for life to contribute my personal knowledge and experience of being the mother of a special needs child to positively impact the lives of many through my ministry. I'm especially excited about how Moses is growing, and developing mentally and emotionally and how he's taking me along with him. I can hardly contain my excitement about the future. I've learned to take one victory at a time, but that way, I'm able to enjoy each one and hold them to my heart even longer.

I am loving life for the first time in my life. No one else can tell me that I can't fulfill my dreams because I'm past what they think is the age limit. We're never past the age limit, unless we think we are. Those are the thoughts of losers and I, and all the other mothers of special needs children, are anything but losers."

For Jennifer a major part of her victory is no longer feeling like a victim.

"For the longest time, I felt sorry for myself, but now I'm O.K. I've also been blessed with a very supportive and loving husband who makes sure that I get a break every year from the stresses of raising Nancy. He takes very good care of us and it makes me cherish our 25 years of marriage even more.
My helping other mothers new to this type of challenge is a major part of my victory over my self pity. They must learn to overcome their own self pity, and they'll come out winners in the end, and I'm grateful to be able to show those mothers how to do it.

It's so important that women with special needs children not compare themselves to other mothers without special needs children.

And mothers without special needs children certainly can't compare what it's like to care for and raise ours. Every situation is unique. Understanding this was a major hurdle for me to overcome and something that I learned not to do to myself anymore. It was hurting me, rather than helping me.

There's a time to cry and there comes a time when your tears dry. Our children all have their own personalities, identities and their own victories. We need to let them be who they are, because it's important for them, and for us.

If there's anything else I could share it is to learn how to choose your battles, because some things just aren't worth fighting over—just don't sweat the small stuff! I'm not saying that we don't give our all into the care and growth of our children, but we have to learn how to take it one day at a time, but recognize what time it is. There's a time to lose sleep and there comes a time to sleep peacefully. There's a time to cry and there also comes a time when your tear wells dry. There's a time to go to battle and there's a time to sit still and wait on the salvation of the Lord.

There is a lot of joy out there, but you have to look for it, and be determined to find it. I had to look for it, but I did find it and in the process found that it is so much better if we all find a way to shout about the victory, not about the fight!

Debbie wholeheartedly agrees with Jennifer, in that she no longer wanted to be the victim, but the victor.

"I grew up and became more mature as a result of parenting my son, Terrance. When I stopped feeling sorry for myself, it seems that my life radically changed spiritually, mentally and even physically. I learned that I couldn't run away from this difficult task and that the only way to get to the top of the mountain was to go through the valleys.

My son, Terrance is such a smart, sensitive and insightful young man. He taught me a valuable lesson through all of this, and that is not to look too far ahead, because tomorrow had its own set of issues to deal with, but we can't be afraid of the future either. He taught me to enjoy each day with my family and to enjoy his successes, as well as my own.

Now I can personally attest to the fact that although it didn't look like it, the future is moving ahead and it's going to be fine. Of course, it is all difficult to accept at first, but eventually there comes a time when the pain subsides, our hearts start to beat again, the sun starts to shine and the rainbows appear.

Parenting our special children and seeing them make small, but major victories of their own, brings about an incredible feeling of joy. It's hard to describe, unless you've been through it—but after you've gone through so much, it's a joy you appreciate, cherish and you never lose, and I thank God for that.

It's time that heals all wounds and for those who give up the fight without even trying, they really don't know what they're missing. You can believe that not only do our victories come from seeing how far we can go with nothing but our faith, but also how far our faith can take us into our victories."

Elizabeth's personal victory was learning that she could trust living again, and that life and most importantly God, had not forsaken her.

"What happened to Jada really shook my confidence and faith in everything and everyone. I was always a believer in God, but in this instance, I was more than a little angry that He would let this happen to me. But after a while, God showed us how much he loved us, by sending us people who cared about us, including total strangers.

It was awesome to see God's light shine through the people He sent to help us get through a difficult time—people we didn't even know. It was as if he blessed us with angels. . In a way, this was my own miraculous experience, seeing God move like I never have before—through people.

I remember that after Jada first went into the coma, as you can imagine, we were too bereaved to even deal with every day life matters. Taking care of our home and even our other two kids became secondary, I'm not too proud to say.

Some close friends, and even some passing acquaintances, got together and came to help us and we know that it was God that put it on their heart to do it.

We had people cooking meals for the family, picking up our other children from school, and helping them with their homework. They would even come to the hospital picking up our keys and would thoroughly clean our house for our parents' visit.

When we did leave the hospital, there was nothing left to do but rest. It was amazing, and even though I didn't realize it at the same time, it was an incredible blessing. We were so out of it, we didn't think people could be so genuine, so sincere, so caring, however, they all turned out to be anchors for us in a time when we needed it most and many of them still serve as rocks to stand on today.

As the many days and months passed, with the encouragement of others, I learned how to start taking care of myself again. I had lost a tremendous amount of weight, I no longer wore make up, and basically, I looked like a hag and I didn't really care. My friends and family would even try to send me to spas to help me unwind, but I never went.

About six months after Jada left us, I finally decided to take a friend up on an offer to accompany her to a spa for a massage, and it was one of the best things that I could have done for myself and my family.

137

I started to come out of my own coma and began enjoying my other children again. I began to spend some quality time with my husband and taking better care of myself. I admit, this took a few years, but eventually I learned that totally giving up on myself, and my family's future was not going to help any of us.

So I started over again. I started eating again, wearing a little makeup, exercising to relieve stress and began to take on some new challenges that would help me to grow. I took on the challenge of learning how to use a computer and actually began to write, putting down my visions for the future on paper.

Instead of wallowing in self pity, I focused on the great times I had with my daughter, from the time she was born until we found out about her tumor. The whole situation made it even more clear to me, that you never know what's around the corner, so you'd better enjoy life and share your love with those close to you everyday.

I'm so grateful that we had such a great relationship with our daughter, and she knows even now, how much we loved her. As we all moved forward, I realized that I had to remember I had two other kids to raise-- a son and another daughter and I had to continue to not only love, cherish and appreciate them, but see to their future happiness. And in the process see to mine and my husband's happiness, as well.

I guess that was my own personal victory, to be

able to even think about anything other than Jada and the pain we all suffered through during these trying last few years. It took a while—a long while, but I began to see the stars behind the clouds, and it was then that the words "live, love, laugh"—words Jada used to always say to me-- took on a whole new meaning. I am now more than ready to do just that, because I realize like I never did before, that life is so precious and can be so short.

And even though I know she's among heaven's angels, Jada will always be in our hearts and I feel her loving spirit, along with the holy spirit surrounding us every day and believe me, that does bring me joy every morning."

As shared earlier, Kate is a typical woman with goals and ambitions, likes and dislikes, and a woman who's won many a battle. Born with cerebral palsy, the mother of an adult son, a grandmother, a college graduate, an influential community leader for the disability community, a corporate executive, a world traveler, an author and an award winning athlete in competitions geared to the disability community, Kate has proven that in many ways, she is atypical. Her whole life is a victory, and we can learn quite a bit from her.

"I believe my life has been a testimony, as well as an example, that no one should put boundaries on other people, or even set limits on themselves. I grew up in the early sixties and as a teenager, people like me were placed in a box—others in the

"system" believed we couldn't do anything, so they never thought to give us a chance.

We weren't valued as people who had enough intelligence to be educated. We also weren't considered to be a contributing part of the community, and we weren't encouraged or empowered enough to become independent—to be more than we were and all that we could be. Back then, and even in some cases today, many of us were institutionalized unnecessarily and I personally know some who were.

Today, we are still fighting to help change that perception, so that those in institutions can be given a chance to live independently. Thankfully, in many cases we are winning and little by little more physically and mentally challenged, but capable people, are coming back into the community. Having a part in that accomplishment and supporting these people to be more than even they thought they could be, is what I've lived for my whole life.

I want to help people with disabilities to enhance their special gifts and talents to afford themselves and their families the best life possible, and that continues to be a major victory for me.

In a time when things are in some cases getting worse than they are getting better for the disability community, I'm thankful that I have an ability to speak up for our community, to communicate our needs to legislators, and serve as a voice until the changes come to fruition.

I believe in passing on my blessings and I try to do that in many ways. I have the ability to learn, so I try to teach and empower others to learn. If I've been blessed to have a positive attitude, it's because of my attitude about life that I have been able to come this far. I make sure I take the time to celebrate all my victories, because they set a standard for those coming after me. Those victories let them know that they can accomplish many wonderful things, but they just have to fight for those things, as I did.

Living life to its fullest makes everyone enjoy their lives even more, and although many look at my challenges as obstacles, I look at them as victories. As I said before, I've been able to accomplish some things that many people without disabilities have yet been able to achieve and I'm proud of that.

Also, I am blessed to see humor in everything. I see the good in everybody and the desire to continue to be the best that I can possibly be tends to transcend to others, something else in which I'm extremely proud.

As I look into the future, I see great opportunities to improve in many areas of my life and teach others to do the same—whether physically or mentally challenged, or not. Everyone should be able to grow intellectually, financially, spiritually, even emotionally. Everyone should be able to enjoy every aspect of their lives because there's no reason not to. Though there were many in my youth and even in my adulthood, who never

141

thought it could happen, look at me now, I have a great job, a great son, a great granddaughter, and a great family---I have it all.

Life is not over until God says it's over—not for any of us and here I am in my 50's and after being married twice, I'm still looking to find the love of my life...I know he's out there somewhere! I haven't even given up on that. My victory is to instill my joy for life in everyone and I'm blessed to have been assigned to do it!"

"The power to walk through valleys, scale many mountains and remove any obstacles is buried within all of us...our victory comes when we recognize it, believe it, receive it and act on it."

CONCLUSION

Elected ladies are like chameleons, we adapt to the environment in which we are placed. As I hope I was able to share through my own life and through the lives of others, being a mother of a child with physical and mental challenges definitely has its highs and lows. But as women who are sometimes misunderstood, we are also intelligent, independent, strong, inspirational, long suffering, selfless, humble, faithful, helpful, loving, full of wisdom and vision. I guess the greatest hidden gift of any mother, is our ability to focus and thrive on the highs and not the lows.

We must remember that we are all on assignment and that God chose each of us especially to fulfill this very special position. As mothers of special needs children, our lives are a little more challenging, but God knew we were up to the task.

All those seeds sown during those many long years of seemingly unending pain will reap tremendous harvests in our lives as we move forward. I want to encourage all elected ladies to look past whatever difficulties you may have experienced, look up to God for help and look forward excitedly to what's ahead.

If you get nothing else from this book, I hope

I've shared with you that we do have choices, to make of our lives as blessed as we would have our lives to be. However, where we focus will tell the tale of where we will end up.

Instead of focusing on what we think is the bad break we believe we've gotten in life, remember what the word in the bible says, to "think on these things that are good, pure and of a good report." I hope you know, as I do, that there are many, many things of which there is a good report.

Our children are not in any way meant to be curses in our lives, but tremendous blessings. There is much more to the reason that they're with us, born the way they were, than what we think or see. God knows all about this challenge and on-going fight, because He allowed it, He gave it to us.

So continue to take the enemies of disbelief, despair, depression and devastation out of your minds and out of your lives. Never stop pushing past and pressing through, because sometimes the greatest battles of our lives are right before the greatest victories. Take heart, take hold and take heed. Your child is your champion, your misery is your ministry and your future is fantastic. The best is yet to come.

God Bless!

MY PRAYER FOR YOU

You are so precious to me
Your life has always been the key
Your smile so bright, in you God's light
Your love so strong, you know no wrong
Train up a child the way they should go
My strength comes from the fact that I know
God has a plan to place you far above
Pressing on through trials with our love
So my prayer for you is
To be the best that you can be
And my prayer for you is
To light the way so we can see
Your love for all is pure, your purpose is sure
But most of all, you led us to God's call
We take so much for granted
In your shoes, could we stand it?
For, there but for the grace of God go we
So my prayer for you is,
To walk into your destiny
And my prayer for you is,
To find true love abundantly
Your love for all is pure, your purpose is sure
But most of all, you led us to God's call

Printed in the United States
75304LV00001B/220-264